FORMS OF EDUCATION
space for contemporary teaching

Giovanni, Marco Chiri
with texts of
Paolo Calidoni, Giovanni Battista Cocco, Massimo Faiferri,
Ferdinando Fornara et al.,
Foreword by Bruno Messina

My initial idea was for this book series to be in one way or another "essential". My opinion was that I could have guided it and developed at least a few of the topics covered in it, only on the condition that it would be truly useful. But useful to whom? Who would really feel the urge to read these short, printed texts? Certainly I didn't – and still don't – have the ambition to contribute substantially to the theory of the project nor to elaborate on themes that are so eccentric that they raise the interest and curiosity of only a few academics in the field. On the other hand, I admit that the mere idea of writing one – or more – strictly educational texts bored me.

Returning to the basis of the discipline and using them to rebuild a way of working has, in a way, a fundamental value and – though this may seem audacious – is highly exciting.

GMC

FORMS OF EDUCATION. Sulla scuola
by Giovanni, Marco Chiri

With texts of Paolo Calidoni, Giovanni Battista Cocco, Massimo Faiferri, Ferdinando Fornara et alt.
Images of Spaziozero e Canargiu-Montis

Foreword by: Bruno Messina

foreword
by Bruno Messina

"I think of school as an space environment of spaces where is good to learn. Schools began with a man under a tree who did not know he was a teacher, discussing his realization with a few who did not know they were students. [...] the entire system of schools that followed from the beginning would not have been possible if the beginning were not in harmony with the nature of man".

Louis Kahn

"I think of school as an space environment of spaces where is good to learn. Schools began with a man under a tree who did not know he was a teacher, discussing his realization with a few who did not know they were students. [...] the entire system of schools that followed from the beginning would not have been possible if the beginning were not in harmony with the nature of man".[1]

LK

A vast heritage and yet inadequate to meet the needs it is called upon to fulfill. This situation is, in summary, the state of the art of Italian school building from any perspective one tries to evaluate it: in terms of seismic safety, eco-sustainability and, above all, functional coherence concerning the new teaching strategies that inform the world of education. It is a bleak picture, tangible testimony to how much inattention politics has given to a front on which the future of our country is played out. The tragedies that had a profound emotional impact across the nation were not enough to drastically reverse a trend that would have required decidedly more incisive interventions than those registered in recent years. The competitions of ideas, announced by the Ministry of Education with the title "Innovative Schools" or the project "Iscol@", promoted by the Autonomous Region of Sardinia, represent a first concrete sign of desire for a change, an effort to give back to Italian educational institution the centrality that belongs to it by right. The path to take cannot but start from the upgrade of the existing school, and the creation of new structures, two necessary and complementary actions to systematically tackle the problem of school construction.

In a territory such as Italy with high seismic risk, the first action, essential and which cannot be postponed, concerns the adaptation of existing schools to energetic and seismic standards, a fact that requires a careful evaluation of the cost-benefit ratio based on quality and state of buildings. The second step is more complex in many ways: the design of new schools and the functional adaptation of existing ones. The typological layout of the traditional school, in fact, based on the idea of the centrality of the classroom as a pedagogical unit, connected to the other rooms by the system of the corridor serving spaces, is hardly adaptable to current teaching strategies that presuppose a flexible organization, capable to provide spatial arrangements open to several modes of use over time.

These strategies, a legacy of the achievements of experimental pedagogy of the 20th century, have found, since the 1950s, exciting areas of experimentation, as in the case of the projects of Hans Scharoun, Ettore Sottsass, Herman Hertzberger or others, cited in the present volume. In these examples, we see continuity between interior and exterior in which the disposition takes shape in an organic sequence of open spaces that refers to the relationship with the city and the landscape. It is a configuration of places where the atmosphere of the spaces establishes a direct link between students' emotional experience and the domain of memory, which is a fundamental condition in learning processes.

Giuseppe Vaccaro's kindergarten in Piacenza and the schools of Aldo Rossi are, in this sense, concrete examples of how the elementary and symbolic character of the primary forms of the architecture of the school constitutes an important perceptive device of identification, learning, and memorization of experiences.

The contributions contained in this volume move from this scenario to question the role that the architectural project can play in the radical rethinking of spaces for education, imposed first of all by the genetic mutation that the web is determining, not without shadows and yet inevitably. A process described by Alessandro Baricco in a recent essay[2] that investigates the invisible boundary line that separates us from the generation of digital natives. Baricco understands the risks deriving from a progressive dematerialization of cognitive processes and human relations and hopes for a return to a new humanism, in the belief that the artificial web life can be, in the end, unnatural for most human beings. And this last consideration on our current condition leads us to look to the future, returning to reflect on the original meaning of the school as an institution and place where the child experiences for the first time his status as *zoòn politikòn*. The return to the beginning which was prophetically advocated by Louis Kahn in 1960.

BM

---

[1] L.Kahn, *The Voice of America*, (1960), trad.it in L.Kahn, *Forma e progettazione*, in V.Scully, Louis I.Kahn, George Braziller, New York, 1962, p. 115
[2] Cfr. A.Baricco, The Game, Einaudi, Torino 2018

index

4
Foreword

13
The school in the middle

33
The landscape as a learning environment

51
Psychological effects of school design attributes

61
Learning spaces, places and landscapes

81
Symbolic and functional over time

90
Bibliography

92
Credits

94
Carnet

> "We shape our buildings, and afterwards, our buildings shape us"
>
> — Winston Churchill

CHAPTER ONE

FORMS OF EDUCATION

Chapter one

The school in the middle

In 2015, Italian law number 107 instituted the "School building data portal" which made images depicting the conditions of the nation's schools available for the first time. The statistics portrayed a bleak situation. About 65% of Italy's schools was built before 1976 (12.7% before 1946) and only 10% after 1991. Of approximately 40,000 school buildings, over 50% (average) necessitate urgent or very urgent maintenance work to comply with earthquake regulations and energy efficiency and safety requirements. In reality, recent national and regional regulatory measures have been numerous and important, funding more than 21 different initiatives with over 9.5 billion euros. In many regions, these resources were used to fully restore a large number of buildings in contexts often burdened by widespread and severe social and economic decay. This support may appear to be little more than a drop in the bucket if we consider, for example, the rate at which work on buildings in earthquake zones (532 on more than 15,000) has been carried out, it would require 113 years to guarantee safety conditions in the highest risk areas. Similarly, it would take about 160 years to bring buildings up to current energy codes. Therefore, even if a program exclusively devoted to the recovery of existing buildings were to be funded with the same intensity, it would take well over a century before they would comply with current standards. At that point however, the older buildings would be two hundred years old, well beyond the life cycle of many of the materials with which they were originally built. Of the total available funding, about 95% is used for renovations (repairs and regular and special maintenance) while the construction of new schools accounts for the residual 5%.

Nevertheless, new school buildings are what is really needed. Although existing schools can be made accessible and safe, they are - and will continue to be – increasingly obsolete in terms of their functional, typological and spatial characteristics. This anomaly is due to the fact that tremendous resources are mostly used to renovate structures that are no longer fully fit for their purposes, unsuitable for today's profoundly changed teaching and learning conditions. Buildings based on outdated ideas (but crystallized in the norms and forms of the 20th century school) must support processes driven by a 21st century society. This contradiction mirrors an image of a nation that does not want to meet the challenge of a future vision; a nation blocked by red tape and extremely lengthy administrative procedures, which are maintained even when they should be innovated.

Some meritorious measures, like the series of national design competitions for "Innovative Schools" and the regional "Iscol@" program in Sardinia, have been effective but are alone insufficient to reverse the conditions in most Italian educational institutions. The inadequacy of the funding available for the widespread reconstruction of the nation's schools means that most of the more recent achievements are virtuous but sporadic cases, too small in number to deeply influence the physiology of the nation's schools. However, for many years to come, the soft underbelly of Italian educational institutions will still be made up of buildings constructed decades ago and renovated several times to adapt to standards and safety parameters, but still (mostly) unsuitable to meet the needs of a profoundly changed educational context.

The shift in educational strategies from teacher to student has produced a reversal of the most commonplace languages of spatial organization and design. Architectural experiments have explored an infinite range of spatial solutions, all in search of typological innovation for learning contexts. Sometimes educational innovation finds its application in new structures built expressly for that purpose but in most cases, at least in Italy, it is shoehorned into the adaptation and reuse of spaces based on a different educational model. So, for example, when corridors are sufficiently wide, they are also used as spaces for recreation, meeting and informal activities along with traditional circulation. What were once atriums become commons, theatres, temporary laboratories, gyms become auditoriums and civic centres. Outdoor spaces are made available to host neighbourhood events after school hours. While waiting to overcome emergency conditions, most Italian schools will be made up of unclear, hybrid spaces, minimally adapted to new needs. Aside from the basic maintenance of structures and mechanical systems, most measures will involve limited spatial reconfigurations, small and medium-sized additions, chromatic modification of vertical and horizontal surfaces, and new furnishings. School buildings will remain in a sort of timeless limbo between "how they were" and "how they want to be".

Even the Italian regulations, at the time of the writing of this text, reflect this intermediate condition. The code regulating most schools is the Ministerial Decree dating from December 18, 1975; it is entitled "Updated technical standards relating to school buildings, including the indicators for educational, building and urban planning functions to be observed in the execution of school building works". A careful reading shows that the text is surprisingly modern. Many of the principles contained in current documents such as "flexibility", "adaptability",

Nursery school in Savogna d'Isonzo
The entrance

"versatility", "transformability of learning and study spaces", as well as the emphasis on the centrality of "special" social and laboratory spaces, had already been addressed extensively in the law. This makes it difficult to affirm that the inadequacy of the buildings constructed under this law depends exclusively on bad legislation. On the other hand, the text is still firmly anchored to an idea of the school organized around the pedagogical unity of the classroom, the traditional educational context. The technical appendixes and charts indicating the minimum floor area requirements for the functional programs of schools have been the only references for decades, stifling any design freedom. New ministerial guidelines tend to invert a "prescriptive" logic in favour of a "performance-based" idea, focusing on places for teaching and learning, their spatial relationships and their role in the learning process, leaving ample liberty for typological, distributive and formal innovation. Technological innovation (IT in particular) is given a central role; it is considered the real game-changer called upon to support and sometimes resolve the shortcomings in current education.

This scenario opens a field of possibilities for design that lies between two opposing extremes. On the one hand is a fairly homogeneous set of school buildings, which, despite the indications in older codes, adapts to educational innovation with extreme difficulty. On the other hand are new projects with new layouts more suitable for the school of tomorrow.

The first of the two prevailing viewpoints in education theory focuses on the figure of an instructor (actor/agent) who delivers teaching to a uniform set of passive subjects (students) whose only task is to assimilate the largest number of concepts possible. The second, perhaps not as important but becoming more widespread, includes a multiplicity of strategies united by placing students and their cognitive abilities at the heart of the process while allowing the instructor to stimulate and activate students' individual potential. Each approach requires a corresponding spatial configuration that ensures goals and results, and if possible amplifies them. Different academic circles still discuss the pros and cons of such models; cyclically one tends to prevail over the other. However friction is generated when a teaching system and its spaces do not correspond, causing evident problems for learning. It also seems true that if an "innovative" educational system (distinguished from the teacher-centred one) faces great difficulties in working in traditional classrooms, the same can be said for the contrary. It is a question that substantially regards compatibility between form and function: correspondence between the processes that must be put into practise and the spaces they must use. This is not to say that there is one method or approach that is better than the other, or that advances in the research on educational strategies are not taken into account. What we want to say is that there are simply no inherently good or bad spaces in and of themselves but only those more or less suitable for specific purposes. Ultimately, in terms of the design of new buildings as well as the re-use of existing ones, there must be coherence between the means and the ends, between the goals and the tools used to achieve them.

This clarification is also necessary to safeguard some architecture of many 20th century schools from the quest for innovation at any cost. In light of new paradigms, these buildings risk having their typological and formal characteristics compromised in order to pursue new methods of teaching and learning. Yet, the fluid matter that is today's science of education does not allow the identification of stable and lasting forms for schools of the future (like so many slogans would have us believe). Let us just consider the changes in learning produced by electronics as early as the late 1980s and 90s, not to mention the impact of smartphones on how we access information today. Perhaps the dematerialization of culture and knowledge within a large, immense cloud of information will not yet make physical places completely superfluous in the transmission of knowledge but it will constantly change those places at ever-more-rapid rates. The idea of crystalizing future learning spaces into specific forms and types is a chimera. It might be possible to work on contemporary phenomena, taking as a premise that inevitable obsolescence is a given in design, thus including a high degree of adaptability in spatial configurations. Therefore, no distinct interpretation or generalizable solutions exist; instead there is a field of application of design that, from time to time, must face its context and times. Based on these assumptions, it might be possible to describe the spatial configurations of the school in a more secular manner without preconceptions or prejudices.

Most school buildings are based on corridor systems along which a series of classrooms is arranged. Each classroom, with the exception of subsequent adaptations, is a regular space organized with rows of desks facing a blackboard and the teacher. In general, windows illuminate the classrooms although their relationship with the exterior does not play a predominant role in its design. The corridor is sized to allow for the rapid flow of students and has no other function. This arrangement corresponds to a model based on the central role of teachers and and the information they must impart. Students are passive recipients whose sole purpose is to focus their attention on the words and explanations of the teacher. Autonomy and

Nursery school in Savogna d'Isonzo
Classroom

Nursery school in Savogna d'Isonzo
The refectory

distraction are discouraged and differences among the students and their cognitive abilities are not taken into account. This scheme regards all academic subjects. In some cases, at the end of a class, the teacher will move to another classroom; in others the entire class moves. Excluding this variant, however, the pedagogical strategy underlying this spatial configuration is the same and tends to consider students (or rather their educations) as products of an industrial process.

The "assembly line" system invented by Frederick Taylor (and readily applied by Henry Ford) was based on the large-scale assembly of products through an ordered sequence of partial actions conducted by a number of workers (actor/agents) having the training strictly necessary for conducting a precise segment of the production process. Similar to the Fordist factory, the 20th school produced an enormous number of literate individuals by means of a simple and relatively inexpensive scheme. Teachers were not required to have any other proficiency beyond their specific disciplines. No interpersonal skills were required since relationships were kept to a minimum. Particular motivational skills and the ability to stimulate individual autonomy were not required since this was discouraged. Consequently, spatial organization was simple. Although this model is now largely outdated, it is still the most prevalent the world over. The passivating approach of providing superficial factual knowledge conflicts with today's availability of instantaneous stimuli, appearing to students as an obsolete and unsuitable approach to the demands not only of the work world but, in general, of contemporary society. Nonetheless it continues to be the standard approach to learning in the school of the masses.

During the 20th century, the theories of those like John Dewey, Jean Piaget, Lev Vygotsky, Maria Montessori and Loris Malaguzzi began to shift attention to a model that placed students, their individuality, the development of autonomy and their active participation in the learning process at the heart of the educational process. This revolution, which was first and foremost cultural and behavioural, could have rapidly supported the school as an institution and as a result influenced the design of learning spaces not only in relation to classroom layout but the overall configuration of the school building. The upending of the classical teacher-student relationship undermined the dominant spatial model.

In the mid-1960s, first in the United Kingdom and later in the United States, the first "schools without walls" were explored. The idea of a single and continuous learning space without the physical barriers of the classrooms and without pre-established hierarchies in desk organization as well as a totally revamped curriculum seemed a promising idea, in keeping with the spirit of the era. However, the radically innovative model soon failed for at least three reasons. The first was that the open space configuration, in which two hundred or more people were to study, relax, talk, and do different things, was not applied by the teachers themselves who preferred to divide the single large space informally (using furniture or other movable partitions). The second was a general withdrawal from 1960s and 70s cultural models that came about on several levels in the following years. The third, and most important, was the impossibility of achieving basic learning goals in a space that did not provide quiet zones, areas reserved for refreshment, individual reading, work in small groups, with appropriate acoustic conditions. The utopia of the school without space failed before it was even born. The failure of the two spatial models (the first due to obsolescence, the second due to excessive radicalism) left great room for new expressions on the typological and formal levels between those two extremes.

This is the subject of the design project. So then, what elements define a project so that it can respond to the needs of a school that claims to be truly "innovative"? In general, school designs are evaluated positively if the spaces correctly fulfil their required functions. This means that: classrooms adequately host a certain number of students; corridors are large enough for ordered circulation; canteens and kitchens comply with compulsory hygiene codes; laboratories have the necessary equipment. Yet these are only preconditions for a school to claim quality. Naturally, once the functional goals are achieved, it is of primary importance for the school to become "a learning environment" and not just a "place for learning": a physical space that nourishes, supports and intensifies the scope of teaching, adapting with flexibility to continuous change, a place that is welcoming and able to send positive messages to a community beyond the physical boundaries of the school itself.

Space as a "third teacher" (after students and teachers) soon became much more than a slogan. This concept assumes that school architecture is no longer the mere context for educational activities but is itself part of teaching and learning. The school becomes a place with which to interact, relate and grow harmoniously; a place that can transmit positive messages, transforming compulsory education into a fulfilling and even seductive experience. The characteristics, and their constraints, necessary for the school of the new millennium are therefore far more broad and complex. They do not differ so much in their functional requirements as much as in their layouts, typological articulations and formal expressions. In other words, new educational spaces are invited to be places for learning and entertainment as well as for social and leisure relations; such functions are also projected into the context of the host community. The school is expected to carry out its public, and in a certain sense, "political" functions in the heart of society. These are no longer solely informative activities but, in a more general sense, formative ones. In this context, architecture is called upon to play an even more important role with respect to other urban questions because of the unique ability of the discipline to embody technical and expressive content by creating the best scenario for the cultural, civic and even emotional growth of children and young adults.

However, two preconditions must be met in order for this paradigm shift to become reality. The first consists of adapting legislation (at least in Italy) that, on the one hand, substantially compels designers to move within very limited margins and to prudently replicate 20th century typological models, and on the other, to constantly innovate spatial configurations, questioning some of the most fundamental and still prevalent assumptions. The temporal sequence of these two operations is not unimportant. The design competition, rightly considered the only process that can guarantee transparency as well as innovation in design, must be able to allow contestants to explore the project with as few predetermined typological constraints as possible. Although, as previously mentioned, the legislation seems to be evolving from a prescriptive to a performance-related approach, to date the only legislative reference is a code conceived 50 years ago. Therefore, in most cases, solutions struggle to overcome the "Fordist" scheme by proposing limited reconfigurations, in most cases entrusted to mobile partitions or furnishings.

The "step forward" that school buildings might take through curricular innovation (with the support of technology) is still greatly limited with disappointing results. In truth, it must be added that even if the regulatory obstacles were completely removed and professionals were finally able to truly explore the limits of school design, the very structure of education may not be ready to receive such innovation. EuroStat 2015 data indicates that, in Europe, the oldest teachers are found in Italy; 57.2% is older than fifty as compared to the European average of 36%; teachers over the age of 60 count for more than 18% as compared to the European average of 9%. With an even older retirement age, this number is destined to increase. It should be noted that the value of experience or skill is not under discussion here. However it is difficult to imagine that radical change in teaching - regarding all aspects of education from the physical to the immaterial - can be brought about by people with thirty or forty years of consolidated behaviours and beliefs that generate conservatism and distrust of all forms of novelty.

The process now underway will take time to produce results that will not always be progressive and linear. Nonetheless, it has begun and learning spaces are gradually changing. Under the pressure of the reforms in curricular strategies and teaching practices, architects today are called upon to rethink the scholastic model at its roots. Leaving aside, for the moment, questions of a regulatory nature that impede true innovation, we focus on the self-imposed limitations of designers who are often unwilling (or unable) to push the limits of their research to the extreme. In other words, preconceived notions act as barriers between architectural design and a fully innovative school in terms of its forms and its processes. Most of the architects who participate in competitions for so-called "innovative" schools studied in traditional buildings, in conventional classrooms connected by circulation spaces most informally adapted to different purposes. The ways in which the various disciplines learned were entirely conventional and neither university studies nor subsequent specializations or refresher courses have changed educational strategies. In these conditions, imagining spaces that are totally alternative to our direct experience is truly difficult: "We build buildings and then buildings build us" (Winston Churchill).

Prakash Nair, considered to be one of the world's leading experts on the subject and who ran a $10 billion program to renovate New York City's schools between 1989 and 1999, suggests starting by changing the names of the spaces, thus compelling people to abandon their entrenched preconceptions. The first operation lies, thus, in rejecting prior conceptual models. The classroom as a "box" exists not only as a physical place but also as a mental space; we might begin by renaming it something like "learning studio" or an intelligent equivalent that no longer expresses the idea of the confining "box" but rather an idea of a space for learning.

The design of a "place for learning" clearly evokes the typological and formal inventiveness of architects more than the normative locution. It is not so much a semantic necessity as much as it is the need to start from processes and create their forms and not vice versa. Based on this viewpoint, design could thus permeate every aspect and detail of the school space, re-discussing the basic premises regarding relationships with the outdoors and green space, the characteristics of the socializing and connective spaces, as well as furnishings and equipment. Experiments and examples in this direction are multiplying daily and it is not important here to mention one or another virtuous example.

On the other hand, it might be more useful to

focus on the four archetypes described by David Thornburg as "primordial metaphors of learning" which, in a certain sense, constitute the groups to which learning spaces are related. The first is the "campfire", which expresses the most traditional system of learning in which there is generally an agent who delivers his/her performative activity (vocal, musical, literary) to other more or less passive subjects. Everything takes place in relatively numerous groups in or around an intimate space. The second archetype is the "watering hole", a place where people occasionally meet in small groups to exchange or share information or to network. The third is the "cave" whose extreme privacy makes it possible to temporarily interrupt social ties and study or rest in full autonomy. Finally there is "life" or direct experience, unmediated contact with real phenomena; in this case, it is not important if activities are carried out individually or collectively as much as learning by performing a task (learning by doing), facing concrete problems and attempting to solve them.

If traditional schools were exclusively made up of "campfire" type spaces, the new generation of schools might have configurations that include spaces of other kinds. The structure, size and form of these spaces depend to a large extent on the availability of space and resources, but in principle it is possible to create, in all conditions (even minimal ones), a small space for networking, for independent learning and even for rest. The objection generally raised is that the floor areas of schools are not sufficient for the multiple functions required of the contemporary school. This is partially true especially when the typological rigidity of some existing buildings does not allow for their optimization or when funding is insufficient. However there is a broad and unexplored field regarding such topics as flexibility, agility and intersections. To be sure, not everything in schools depends on choices made by architects; class schedules and activity planning in general (for example the use of laboratories) do not escape the previously mentioned "assembly line" logic. A careful reading of schedules and the use of teaching spaces (even the most conventional ones) reveals that many are used for a single purpose but are not occupied for the entire school day. This means that the same space - if correctly configured - could be used for different purposes. In other instances, the exact opposite is true, namely that the same kind of activity tends to completely saturate some spaces (for example the classrooms) when it might be better hosted in other places. The optimization of schedules and spaces is certainly necessary as every competent school principal knows, but this concept could be taken to the extreme by involving the physical and organizational structure of the school as a whole. The idea of multiplying spaces for a new concept of teaching and learning was largely misinterpreted as the multiplication of the areas necessary for activities when it might have been the opportunity to invent complex "both-and" spaces. A gym is obviously a gym when it hosts sports activities but with a few adjustments, it can become an auditorium, a commons, a space for group exhibitions, presentations or even a learning studio for very large groups. Traditional classrooms, if adequately outfitted, can be reconfigured in multiple ways to serve a wide array of activities. Generally speaking, no one would prohibit someone from attending a lesson while sitting on a sofa using writing or laptop stands, as I am doing right now, rather than at uncomfortable desks, reducing the distance between the classroom and more informal spaces.

Ultimately it is a question of starting from educational processes and constructing spaces that can support them in the most versatile ways possible, overcoming the temptation to create specialized spaces as far as possible.

In reality, this transformation of the school has a genealogy of its own that can be traced to the transformation of work spaces in the 1980s, especially in the computer industry. The legendary Xerox studio, which inspired Steve Jobs to create Apple and which is still the main reference for the configuration of creative work spaces at many new economy companies, was based on the principle of collaborative and informal learning and working, a concept that is as timely as ever in a world that is increasingly connected and digitally shared. The most radical experiments in school without walls met with very little success as we have seen. On the contrary, the structuring of learning spaces that include the largest possible number of ways to study, work and share results is now a widespread necessity. It is therefore not a question of destructuring space but rather of inclusively re-configuring the multiple activities that can be carried out within any given space. Obviously we cannot expect a gym to function well as a theatre or vice versa, but it is likely that it could perform its function well enough to allow the school to have both a gym and a theatre, and this can be applied analogously to many other scholastic spaces. The advantages offered by the versatility of learning environments might also help schools adapt to the evolution of learning methods. If the classic frontal lesson was already overcome in the last century by a learning-by-doing approach, by cooperative learning and by other forms of teaching, it is possible that in the near future, technology can offer new opportunities to change the ways we learn. Moreover, because education should not try to keep up with the (ever more profound and rapid) transformation of society, it also cannot fail to do so, because if it did not, it would risk losing contact with the evolution of contemporary phenomena, condemning entire generations to being unable to manage them.

The impacts that new technologies have had on education are certainly important but not as much as on other aspects of society. Paradoxically, teaching methods were not particularly influenced by the pervasive use of personal computers, the internet, smartphones and now digital fabrication. Technology is generally underutilized or even demonized by most teaching staff with the exception of the most advanced technological institutes. Personal computers, accessible to the masses since the late 1980s, have been relegated to "computer laboratories" instead of being fully integrated within everyday learning activities. The internet, which has become the daily companion for all kinds of activities (from social to recreational to work-related) for people from five to fifty, plays a very marginal role in schools when it is not merely viewed with suspicion or aversion. The same fate awaited the hardware designed for multimedia education that would (in its initial intents) subvert traditional schooling but which, in fact, remains unused or underutilized. Even the digitization of paper content that can be downloaded to a tablet or a Kindle has not countered the perpetuation of the printed word. Resistance to the use of technology can largely be attributed to the time frames within which schools can profoundly renew educational processes. So while each of us normally has a device to access to knowledge, interact, share content and information in real time, the applications of those same technologies in schools are still perceived as somewhat avant-garde. This generates a detachment of the school, as it is perceived by its users, from the real world. "Digital natives" are much more experienced in the use of computer devices than their teachers and are also enormously more dependent on them. The temporary deprivation of technology distances students from content and experiences and, ultimately, from learning. The process of embedding information technology in schools (and, I might add, universities) should be fully achieved by making the education process as natural as the common activity of networking.

However, in an era of Big Data, the expression commonly used to define the enormous (almost infinite) amount of data and information constantly generated and accumulated in the digital universe, if schools were completely open to this transformation they could be revolutionized. When, at the beginning of the 2000s, some school libraries in the United States began to digitize their collections, paper seemingly became useless. The same came about for newspaper libraries, record and photo collections and to a lesser extent art collections. The physical space for accessing knowledge was thus, first and foremost, the "media library": a "bridge" between physical and digital space. However, in a short time even this spatial form became obsolete with the inexorable advancement of on-demand content on handheld media and customized with no regard for the physical location of the user. The school library (and then the city library) thus became a useless collection of perishable objects and was soon converted for other uses.

When architects were discussing the role of large shopping centers in the space of the contemporary city until just over twenty years ago, no one could have said that in less than two decades they would not only have lost their roles as places for social relations but that their very *raison d'être* would have disappeared with the growth of global online shopping. Thus the mega-malls, which largely determined the modification of the space and landscape of the so-called "advanced" nations as early as the 1950s, are inexorably closing down in the United States due to the prevalence of new forms of commercial distribution.

Analogously, what will be said about school space when educational content will be provided exclusively on-line (tutorials, e-learning, TED etc.), when the space for cooperative learning will be made efficient and less impersonal (for example through the use of virtual reality), when social and experiential activities can be conducted regardless of the physical location of the school? Then, those places will have to be re-interpreted or at least relinquish the forms that have defined them thus far. Until then, the school as we known it will remain immersed in a progressive and inexorable renewal of its forms and meaning.

GMC

Nursery school in Savogna d'Isonzo
The lobby

"The work is not only
the object, but also
what surrounds it
and the gaps, the spaces"

Oscar Niemeyer

CHAPTER TWO

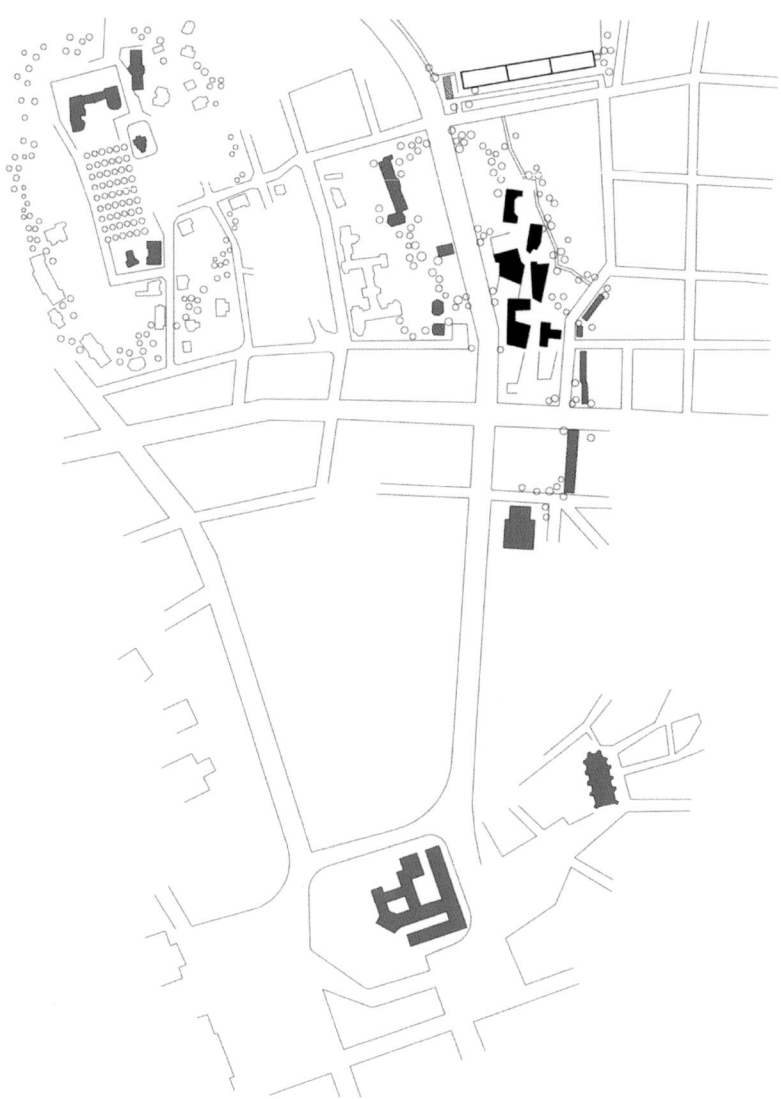

Hans Scharoun, Elementary School in Darmstadt.
Planimetry

Chapter two

The landscape as a learning environment

Over the past four years, the rehabilitation of school buildings in Italy has been high on the national political agenda, through multiannual action plans to improve the existing facilities and construct new buildings, the aim being to develop 'innovative spaces' to accommodate the constant evolution of teaching practices. To pursue this aim, the national programme "*La Buona Scuola*" (The Good School) was launched under Law 107/2015 "Reform of the national education and training system and delegation of powers to reorganise the existing legal framework", with a budget of EUR 4 billion, to improve the safety of 36,000 schools and build at least one 'innovative school' in each region. In line with the national action plan, the Sardinia Region has launched the "Iscol@" programme: an extraordinary plan for renovation of the Region's schools, to make school facilities more efficient, improve their quality and bring them into line with current educational needs. The project, launched by Regional Decree no. 10/15 of 2014, comprises three strands: the first, "Schools of the New Millennium", concerns the construction of new school buildings; the second, "Safety upgrades, minor extension and routine maintenance of school buildings", aims to improve the quality of existing facilities; the third concerns the purchase of new furniture and teaching equipment. By this plan, the Region of Sardinia intended to improve the delivery of education in its territory, also by upgrading or constructing facilities meeting the needs of today's teaching and learning processes, and to root schools in their local communities, giving back to schools and their architectural quality the central role they had long lost. This set of measures has produced a national-level laboratory for developing experimental projects, building on the policy lines developed in previous years. The focus is on the landscape as a matrix for continuing education and, consequently, semiotic space, i.e. awareness of the two-way relationship between architecture and learning approaches. Thus, the project actions focus on the importance of the context for learning outcomes. The contexts are not mere sets for the learning experience but, as observed by Paola Granata, they are in themselves places that help to shape those experiences in a two-way, back and forth process. This awareness is not recent, but ties up with many experiences that all along the 20th century highlighted the link between architecture and education.

The view of the city as a wider classroom is a theme that from the late 19th century to the present was fostered by the active learning theories inspired first by Rousseau and later

by John Dewey, and by the 'new education' models revolving around the pupils, instead of the syllabi, and helped to mitigate the old conflict between closed and open space. The separation between the indoor and outdoor environments was particularly evident in the 'Mammoth schools', the name given in the early 20th century to German schools consisting of aligned blocks with a central, non-ventilated corridor onto which the classrooms opened, using the building's double exposure. School buildings gradually lost this 'compressed' layout and became more permeable to outdoor spaces and their use.
Starting from the 'Copernican revolution' brought about by Rousseau, albeit with different interpretations, the concept of active learning gave teachers the role of coordinators of the transmission of knowledge. Thus, the entire organization of the 'educating community' was put at the service of this role. Several effective slogans were coined to describe this approach: "a school that is not a school", "learn through play", "a school desk that is not a desk". Thus, after the two early innovative experiences of the syllabi approved by Decree no. 549 of 24 May 1945 (which replaced the Fascist authoritarian teaching model laying emphasis on self-management and self-discipline) and of the syllabi approved in 1955 by Presidential Decree no. 503 of 14 June 1955 (inspired by the approach of Belgian educator Ovide Decroly), Italy too embarked on a path of radical change of its educational facilities and models. Under the difficult circumstances caused by the war and the post-war reconstruction period, in which the concept of size, for instance, was seen only in quantitative terms as the number of classrooms, similarly to the focus on the number of rooms in modern dwellings, the need was recognised to conceive an integrated education system were all the different places of learning could deliver their full potential, be they formal (schools, universities etc.), non-formal (associations, the oratory, ...,) or informal (the square, the cinema, ...,). "The design of traditional teacher-centred schools did not place particular demands on designers, other than to ensure a healthy environment. But the school focused on discovery and cooperation requires specifically designed physical and mental spaces" (A. Visalberghi, 1960:45). In this complex environment, the school, as Neil Postman wrote already in 1968, should act as a 'thermostat': in other words, its role is to provide educational balance. So, as the school opens to the surrounding environment, we rediscover the educational nature of built space, which becomes the expression of a broader space, of the local cultures in which the school community is set.

To apply this model, designers must shift the focus away from the architectural object seen as the ultimate goal of his mission, to explore the ways in which the shape (of the school) interacts with the surrounding territory, estab-

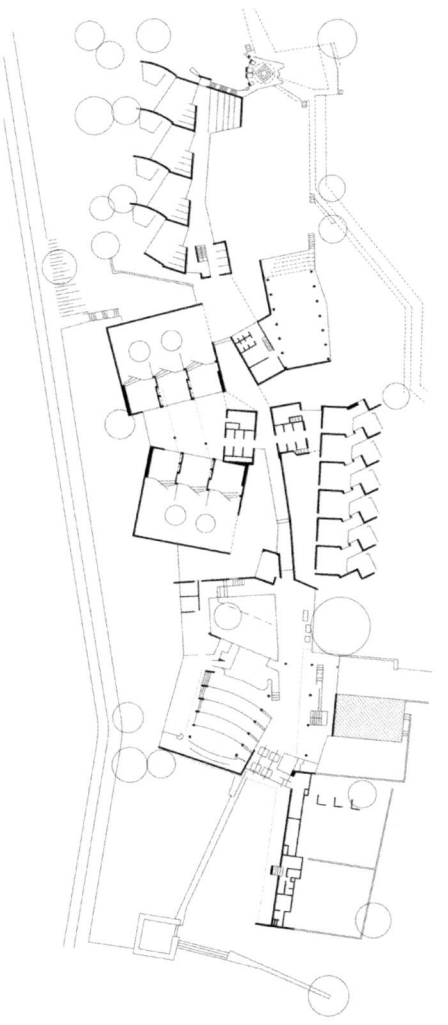

Hans Scharoun, Elementary School in Darmstadt.
Ground floor plan

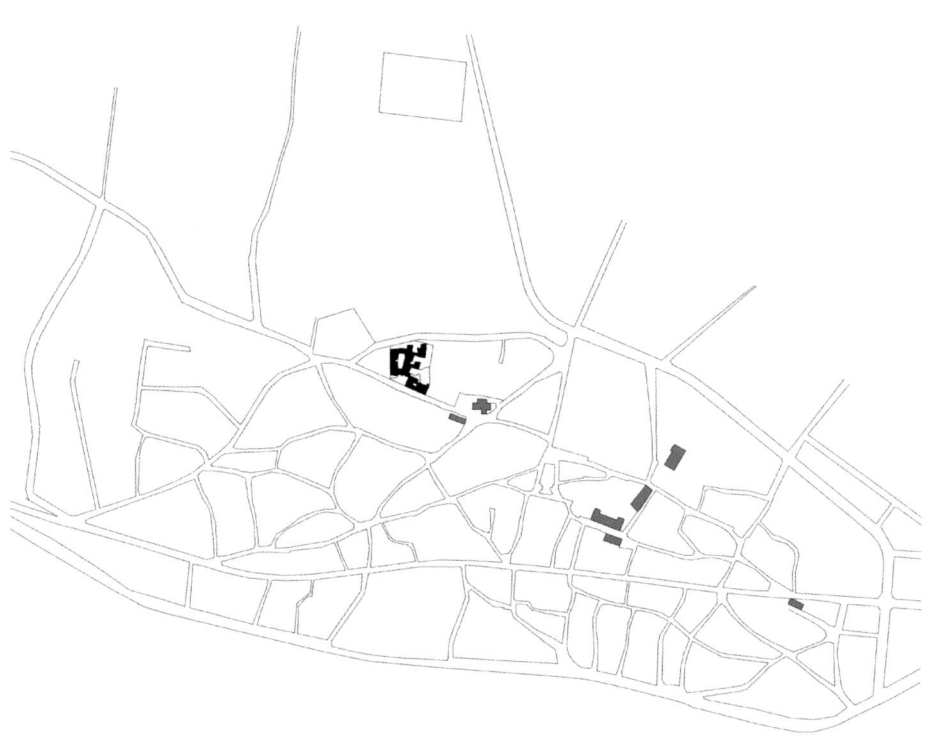

Ettore Sottsass sr., Ettore Sottsass jr., Primary school in Siliqua
Planimetry

Ettore Sottsass sr., Ettore Sottsass jr., Primary school in Siliqua
Ground floor plan

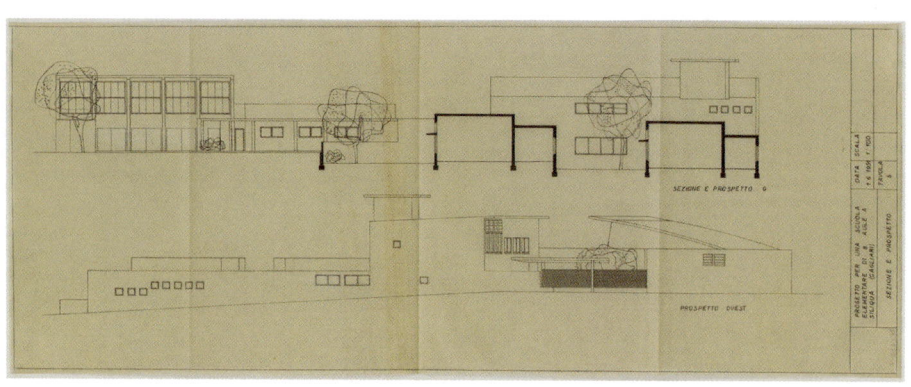

Ettore Sottsass sr., Ettore Sottsass jr., Primary school in Siliqua
Section-elevation G and west elevation

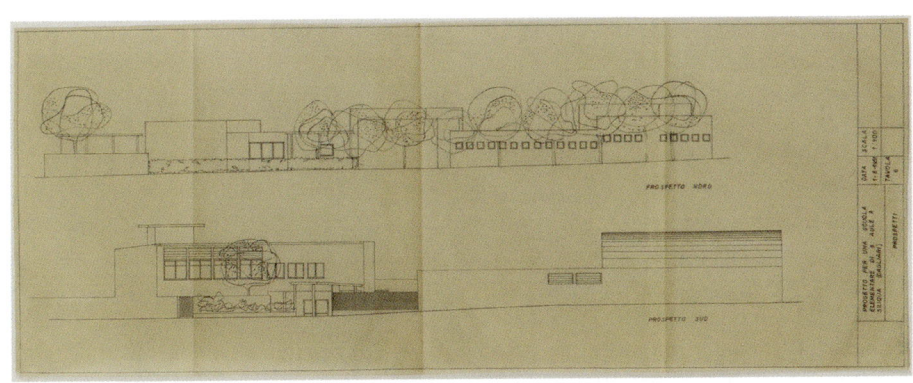

Ettore Sottsass sr., Ettore Sottsass jr., Primary school in Siliqua
North and south elevations

lishing dialogue, rediscovering the individual in his or her emotional and affective dimension (rediscovering the landscape). So, as Luigi Snozzi warned in the seventies, we cannot run away from our responsibilities and we become aware of the fact that by dealing with the shape we can rediscover the human being.

Two cases help us to better understand these issues and to narrow down the field of experimental design discussed in the next paragraph. The first case concerns the primary school that Hans Scharoun presented at the "Man and Space" conference in Darmstadt, directed by Otto Bartning, which attempted to outline an architectural renewal strategy for the post-war reconstruction of Germany. In the conference, which featured some of the main thinkers of the time, such as Ernst Schweizer, Rudolf Schwarz and Martin Heidegger, Scharoun presented an innovative project for a primary school that 'humanised' architecture, through the varied use of space.

The second case is the primary school designed by Ettore Sottsass sr. for the small town of Siliqua, a commission he obtained through Christian Democrat MP Pietro Fadda, as we read in a letter dated 1950 in the MART Archive of the 20th Century: "(...) In the meantime, Fadda has been preparing the ground to ensure I am awarded the commission to design a school in a town near Iglesias, I'm not sure which, perhaps Siliqua" (Sottsass sr. Fund, Notepads [1949-1953], 30 papers, manuscripts Sot. III.1.9, page 20).

Both projects, which remained on paper only, were drafted in 1951, at a time, which, as is known, marked by a wave of architectural research in Italy and in the whole of Europe. Consider some other interesting projects of the period, such as the small circular project, walled and balanced between interior and exterior, developed in 1953-61 by Giuseppe Vaccaro for the child nursery in the Galleana Unit, a social housing estate in Piacenza. Consider also the many conferences and debates held in those years: the International Congress of School Architecture and Outdoor Learning held in Florence in 1949, which concluded that the modern school should abandon the pavilion structure and should comprise psychologically functional units; the national competition launched in 1952 by the Ministry of Education for the design of schools with three to eight classrooms, requiring close cooperation between designers and teachers, whose results were recorded in Report 2 (primary schools) and Report 3 (kindergarten) on the new approaches to school design, published by the Ministry's Study Centre in 1954; the XII Milan Triennial which in 1960 focused on the theme *Home and School*, continuing the debates previously held in Zurich (1953), Rotterdam (1956), Brussels (1956) and Paris (1959) on the issue of learning spaces.

Scharoun's school is designed as a small 'city', with three 'neighbourhoods' corresponding to three elementary districts: of play (6-9 years), development (9-12 years), spiritual or personality (12-14 years). Each cluster has a common hall and "essential circuits" connected with each other by several relationships between inner space and outer space. This group of classrooms looks onto a common route – the "path of encounter" connecting two other spaces: the communal district, housing the library and rooms for meetings between pupils and between the school and the local community; and the semi-communal district, with the gym and sports facilities. Scharoun's aim was not to create a beautiful building for its own sake but to chart, through the educational value of space, the evolutionary cycle of pupils "from unawareness to full awareness, through the route of understanding and intelligence" (C. Cicconcelli, 1958:904), by reproducing in the school the different relationships people experience daily in a town.

Similarly to the first case, the school in Siliqua, has a complex floor plan: each classroom has its own small outdoor space, surrounded by a high wall and partly covered by a pergola. The eight classroom-garden pairs, linked by covered hallways, form a "varied" and "articulated" figure (E. Sottsass sr., 1955:17) very similar to that of the small Mediterranean villages comprising homes with patios, such as the one imagined in 1953 by Costantino Nivola for his hometown Orani. In Nivola's project, entitled, *The pergola village* – which similarly to the other projects just mentioned was never constructed – the vine-covered pergolas on the labyrinth of streets emphasise the overall purpose of the project, namely to encourage social interactions between the townspeople. Likewise, the alternating wide and narrow sections of the covered walkways in Sottsass' design shape the common spaces so as to promote encounter and social interaction between pupils of different ages, similarly to Scharoun's project. The watercoloured elevation drawings of Sottsass' project are especially interesting. They propose a lively and eye-catching architecture with careful use of materials, rich in surprises, colours and light, revealing clearly the contribution of Ettore Sottsass jr., who wrote about this project: "The colour of the space is not just yellow and red or blue and green, but the colour is light, as we know: so it's also black and white and it is matter, smooth as steel and spongy like bone dried by the sun, tender like wood and hard as granite, transparent as air or heavy like lead: space has a thousand of hues and a thousand of sizes and we take it and throw it in the air. We throw in the air our despair and our happiness, our discovery of the world through this new matter we have just met, this new story, which must be found and cannot remain the old story, because what the world brings to us is speed, that is time in space, that is rhythm, and no one can live outside this story and all humans share the same destiny" (E. Sottsass jr., 2017:122).

The two projects were intended for sites which in the 1950s lay on the edge of the urban area. In both cases, the schools were intended to 'occupy new land', surrounded by wide open spaces, and allowing future expansions in line with the original design and maintaining a fully coherent overall structure. Thus, the two schools interact with the existing urban forms, absorbing their values instead of opposing them with a pretence of autonomy. They take from the built environment the best expression of the social, economic and production context, and offer to the town's life spaces that are designed to balance the autonomy of the school with the ability to interpret the needs of the town. These projects suggest that it is possible to start from the school to reconstruct the landscape and, vice versa, that it is necessary to observe the landscape to envision a 'good school'. In other words – to paraphrase Gramsci – these projects tell us we must study – because the town-landscape will need all our intelligence.

*

Experimental design. The Urban Civic Campus "Gaetano Cima" in Guasila
The refurbishment project for the school district "Gaetano Cima" in Guasila – which includes the schools of the towns of Samatzai, Guamaggiore, Pimentel, Selegas and Ortacesus with a total of 609 pupils is part of the actions funded by the "Schools of the New Millennium" programme (Iscol@, strand I), by which Sardinia is strengthening the interdisciplinary ties between architecture and education, by creating facilities for active learning.

The project – whose preliminary studies were coordinated by the undersigned author and have been developed under the scientific agreement signed between The Council administration and the Civil-Environmental Engineering and Architecture – was developed by bringing together all stakeholders (the school district principal, teachers, parents, the educational psychologist, sports clubs, etc.). The designer's role was to give shape to the needs expressed by this community. The group of stakeholders discussed the educational programme, designing a learning path that consolidates and expands the relationships existing in the territory, identifying specific values of the context, translated into spatial forms. In this dialectic between architecture and landscape, the school plays the role of active participant in reconstructing the context and highlighting its educational potential.

The comprehensive institute at Guasila comprises three school levels: kindergarten, primary and lower secondary school. The project focuses on two existing buildings in the lot bounded by three streets: Scintu,

Eleonora d'Arborea and Manzoni, which also comprises a small auditorium. The area is a large plot in the north-western outskirts of town, where the high-density town centre surrounding the 19th-century church of Beata Vergine Assunta, designed by Gaetano Cima, gives way to a low-density neighbourhood of detached houses on single plots. The first building – a former lower secondary school built in 1969 to a design by Engineer Francesco Nannoi – currently houses on the first floor the school administration offices. The second building – built in 1962 as a primary school – houses temporarily the three school levels present in the district. Slightly to the west, opposite the side overlooking via Eleonora d'Arborea, stand a kindergarten and a small nursing home.

The morphology of this area of the town shows that its development was driven by purely functional needs. Thus, the main focus was on occupying space instead of connecting the various built elements. The school was originally built as a 'container' of activities, leaving the open space as mere residual space, undefined emptiness (mammoth school/compressed school).

The renovation project intends to establish relations between the different elements, in a way that fosters learning and is open to the landscape. The project aims to arrange, measure and rediscover the role of urban architecture in construction of the town.

Classical elements are introduced to pay homage to Cima, an important 19th-century architect who left his mark in Guasila and beyond. At the same time, the project highlights elements of the diverse local culture, paying homage to Giulio Angioni's anthropological studies and to the stories about the heritage of the Sardinian people, their desire for freedom and their hard toil.

The project includes a central route across the building lots, which serves both as a cultural route and as a path of encounter, stretching between two ends of via Eleonora d'Arborea and giving access to the various buildings. This route is the backbone of the civic urban campus "Gaetano Cima": a new urban centre, connecting the school community with the rest of the town and providing the school with spaces and facilities for outdoor learning.

The project covers both the building housing the administrative office and the one currently hosting the classrooms: the former will host the primary school (ground floor) and the secondary school (first floor), including art, imaging and technology workshops. The latter will host on the ground floor the school offices and town council offices, plus a meeting room for teachers' meetings and teacher-parent meetings. The strengthening of the relationship between indoor and outdoor spaces is a leitmotif of the entire project. This is very clear, for example, in the classrooms each with its garden on the

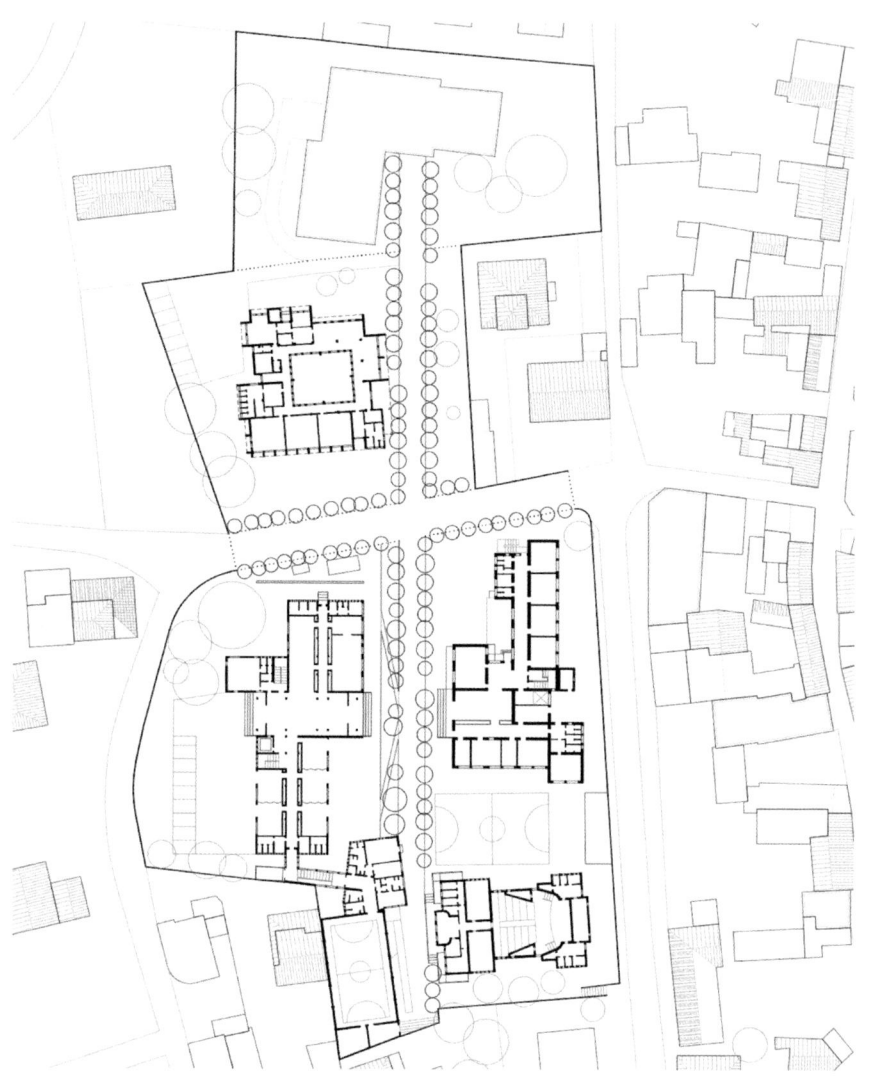

Guasila. "Gaetano Cima" Urban Civic Campus.
Urban plan

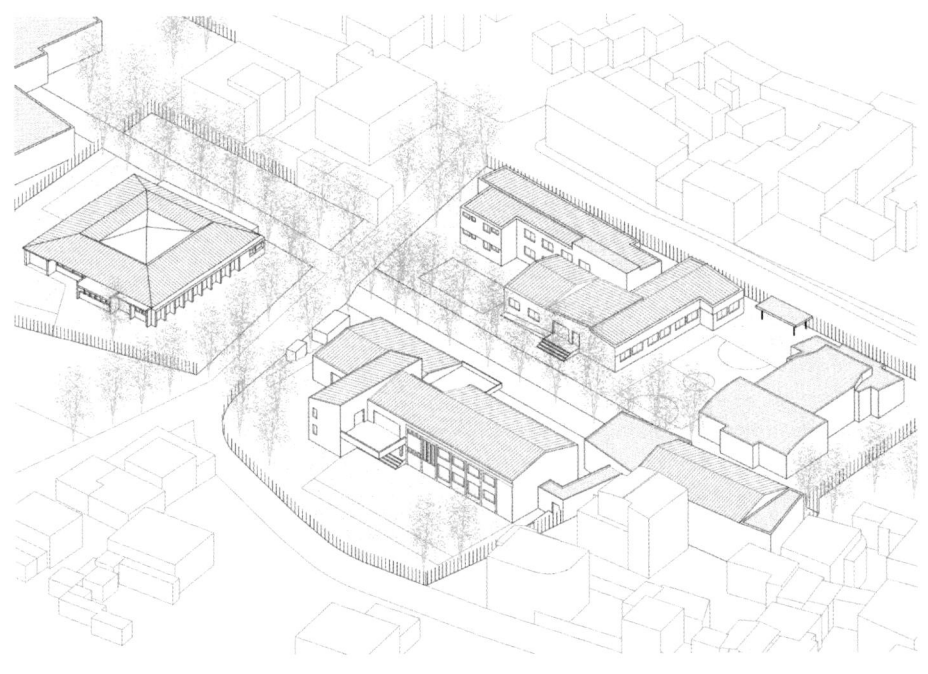

Guasila. "Gaetano Cima" Urban Civic Campus.
Axonometry

ground and first floor of the former administration building, and it is made particularly evident by the central role of the 'Agorà', a public transit space and a meeting place, which links together, without interruption, the open space onto via Manin, with the 'internal' space of the 'path of encounter'. The library, another key element of the educational programme, a place for reading and hearing stories about the multiple cultures mentioned above, is connected with the 'Agorà', to the extent that it is hard to tell where one starts and the other ends. This ambiguity plays an important role in the perception of space, which is conceived as a place for discussion, sharing and rediscovering the dialogic nature of learning. Finally, the classrooms and communal areas are linked to each other by straight hallways, which order and arrange the school spaces, but also serve as spaces for relaxing and unwinding, allowing pupils to experience them as familiar, daily-life places, where they can leave a trace of themselves and their history.

The project revolves around these 'devices', which are also the key to interpreting it. It proposes a precise idea of space – in tune with innovations in teaching and learning practices – to rebuild the forms of the urban landscape. In this sense the school expresses its true essence, eschewing false truths and preconceived models, to rediscover its present-day way of 'being' and 'doing', as an authentic expression of its time.

GBC

"The child has a hundred languages, a hundred hands, a hundred thoughts, a hundred ways of thinking, of playing and of talking to"

Loris Malaguzzi

CHAPTER THREE

Campus Civico urbano Gaetano Cima
Interni

Chapter three

Psychological effects of school design attributes

In recent decades, the relationship between human health and built environment has been broadly studied and has received an increasing attention, in particular through a "user-centred" approach (Gifford, 2002). According to this perspective, spaces should be designed with a focus on the specific needs, preferences, and requests of users who will use certain environments. Thus, it appears clear the necessity to carefully consider the building's physical setting, the psychological characteristics of its users and above all the connection between environment and users.

Healthcare environments have been the focus of many studies in the environmental psychology domain. In particular, the construct of "design humanization" (Fornara et al., 2006; Nagasawa, 2000) refers to those spatial-physical features that influence the individual's behavior. It indicates a set of design features that should be provided to satisfy users' needs (Evans & McCoy, 1998; Fornara & Andrade, 2012; Pressly & Heesacker, 2001), generalizing to other built environments such as residential buildings, offices, or schools. Promoting higher levels of design humanization in a classroom mean to focus on its spatial-physical setting with the main goal to improve the students' performances in terms of both learning and sense of wellbeing. This is particularly relevant if we consider the amount of time spent everyday by students and staff at school.

The design attributes highlighted within the humanization framework recall those "school facility factors" (including quality of maintenance, colors, lighting, noise, temperature, and air quality; Sanoff & Walden, 2012) that influence students' health, safety, sense of self and psychological state. Similarly, in the framework offered by Gifford (2002), humanization design features can be involved in those "physical features of the learning environment" that are variables (besides personal characteristics of the student and social/organizational climate) influencing students' attitudes toward learning (such as desire to learn and satisfaction toward the school experience) and their related behaviours (such as performance and participation/involvement).

Research literature has shown the relevant role of physical features in improving the students' satisfaction and performance. Empirical evidence has been produced about the effects of specific school design attributes on individual and social outcomes, such as state (Earthman, 1999) and dimension of the school facility (Fowler, 1995), noise (Earthman, 2004), temperature and indoor air quality (Norbäck, Torgén, & Edling, 1990), personalization of spaces (Neill, 1982), interpersonal distance (Weinstein, 1979), furniture quality (Gifford, 2014), classroom lighting conditions (Earthman, 2004), spatial layout (Wheldall & Lam, 1987), and presence of natural elements in outdoor spaces (Arbogast, Kane, Kirwan & Hertel, 2009).

In this regard, the majority of the studies have investigated the classroom's design features such as lighting, ventilation, and level of acoustic.

Due to the high level of visual activities, it is important to consider lighting while designing educational spaces, paying attention, especially to natural light. Indeed, daylight seems to have a positive effect on students' learning and concentration (Lee, Kwon, & Lim, 2016), performance (Ahadi, Khanmohammadi, Masoudinejad, & Alirezaie, 2016) and better health (Nilforoushan, Hanna, Naeini, & Mozzafar, 2013) compared to classrooms with artificial light. Another factor showing a positive impact on short-term concentration and performance is ventilation (Petersen, Jensen, Pedersen, & Rasmussen, 2016).

Several studies focused on acoustic features identified noise as a potential factor able to reduce levels of attention and concentration. Specifically, school buildings located at short distance from main roads had a higher level of noise pollution, with a significant impact on students and teachers' performance and comfort (Castro-Martínez, Chavarría Roa, Parra Benítez, & González, 2016). Also, higher noise levels impair memory and learning (Ljung, Sörqvist, Kjellberg, & Green, 2011), even if the extent of annoyance depends on the task (e.g., verbal tasks, and basic mathematics; Brännström et al., 2017). Finally, literature has revealed the impact of noise on conversational interaction showing that higher noise levels impeded the development of interaction and collaborative learning (McKellin, Shahin, Hodgson, Jamieson, & Pichora-Fuller, 2011).

Regarding the impact on users of architectural design, several researches have focused on the influence of the age of the school building (old, new, renovated) on students' performance. A recent study has shown that age of building has a different impact on school leader evaluation of learning environment, with new schools that scored higher than old or refurbished schools in some factors such as aesthetics, ecology, and feelings; and old schools that scored higher than new or refurbished schools in other factors such as creativity, logic and mathematics (Cencič, 2017).

Thus, evidence showed that better building design is associated with higher performance (Lumpkin, 2016), with a positive benefit also on students' wellbeing (Cuyvers, De Weerd, Dupont, Mols, & Nuytten, 2011).

Furthermore, research outcomes have highlighted the importance of the educational environment on students' performance and learning ability. Considering the appropriate size of the building, it was found that facilities should be not too large in order to foster the development of children identity (Slunjski, 2015). According to this study, the presence of too many groups in a kindergarten makes difficult for children to socialize and communicate each other, and such occurrence is also an obstacle to free movement of children throughout the facility. The learning space, indeed, becomes part of students' identity and, in turn, they become part of the place (Wolsey & Uline, 2010).

In order to increase the level of students' performance and satisfaction, several studies have shown the importance of designing classrooms with charming colours, pictures and ergonomic furniture. Specifically, a soft, warm and intimate space is required in order to improve the academic marks (Odole, Odunaiya, Oyewole, & Ogunmola, 2014). Furniture designed for children (e.g., chairs) were also identified as features with a significant impact (Smith, 2013). Levels of satisfaction, wellbeing, and comfort are improved by ergonomic furniture painted with attractive colours and pictures (Maheshwar & Jawalkar, 2014), well-equipped libraries, a sufficient number of classrooms (Odole, Odunaiya, Oyewole, & Ogunmola, 2014), and a fitted blackboard (Martins & Gaudiot, 2012). On the other hand, flexible learning environments with open and transparent designs (e.g., open spaces or interior windows) may have a negative effect on students' attention and sense of privacy (Leiringer & Cardellino, 2011). However, a classroom design with a flexible space promotes self-direct students' learning (Topçu, 2013) and also teachers reported several benefits on students, e.g. increasing engagement with the academic content, retaining information and improving capacity to learn and remember materials (Benes, Finn, Sullivan, & Yan, 2016).

Finally, in order to improve students' performance and wellbeing, evidence suggests also the integration of both indoor and outdoor learning. Recent research has investigated teachers' perception and students' learning in the outdoor learning experience. Indeed, green spaces registered significant positive effects, both in terms of better health and higher engagement in lessons, improving critical thinking skills, problem-solving abilities and enhancing sense of independence, motivation and responsibility (Yates & Sullivan, 2017). Outdoor lessons triggered students' desire to learn in a natural environment (Gomboc, 2016), promoting also children's imaginative play and the development of social positive relationships (Christie, Beames, & Higgins, 2016). Indeed, contact with nature represents both an incentive to learn and a relaxing context able to foster a collaborative relationship between students and teachers (Neilson, 2009). Furthermore, outdoor experience enhanced students' emotional responses (Hanvey, 2010). According to Dhanapal & Lim (2013),

Innovative all-inclusive school North Area. Palermo
The entrance

Innovative all-inclusive school North Area. Palermo
The distribution

an integration of both indoor and outdoor learning is recommended in order to improve students' performance. As regards teachers' perceptions, they positively underlined the impact of outdoor teaching, reporting a whole involvement of students' senses and the resulting enhancement of learning (Gehris, Gooze, & Whitaker, 2015). A better social and personal wellbeing were also reported (Bortolotti, Crudeli, & Ritscher, 2014).

Such empirical findings indicate that the design of an educational environment should pay attention of several school physical attributes, of both internal and external spaces, in order to fit with users' needs and improve learning experiences. Overall, following an "evidence-based design" approach (Hamilton, 2003), these research findings should inform the development of school design interventions, which are expected to promote positive influences on students' engagement, achievement, affective state, comfort and wellbeing, cognitive processes, social interactions, identification with the place, pro-social and pro-environmental behaviour.

In the long term, the downstream results could be the reduction of the number of early school leavers, the increase of wellbeing of students with specific learning disorders, promotion of positive social interactions (e.g., reduction of bullying) and integration (e.g., reduction of ethnic prejudice), and prevention of teachers' burnout.

The recent trends suggest that "classic" old-style schools are likely to disappear in the future replaced by new educational environments. Thus, these literature results can be useful as guidelines for the best practices that professionals such as architects, psychologists, education scientists, teachers, policymakers and members of the community could share within a "user-centered design" perspective (Gifford, 2002).

FF *et al.****

***Sara Manca, Veronica Cerina, Clara Carreras, Simona Sacchi, Valentina Tobia and Ferdinando Fornara

Innovative all-inclusive school North Area. Palermo
The distribution

"Every space could be used as a learning place"

Colin Ward

CHAPTER FOUR

Innovative all-inclusive school North Area. Palermo

chapter four

Learning spaces, places and landscapes

«Every space could be used as a learning place. From early childhood children learn from the environment surrounding them, observing their parents and those close to them, carefully watching, then copying how they do their work. But since labour moved from home to factory, this unconscious learning provided by the domestic environment has been replaced by deliberate teaching in designated places which today we call schools» – Colin Ward

Colin Ward explains that one of the characteristics of the human species is an incessant spontaneous urge to learn that accompanies us from the earliest days of life in every circumstance and context. The environment is undoubtedly able to mediate the learning process and strongly condition it, but it is equally certain that this inescapable need progressively wanes when it is organised and enclosed within structured, restricted organisations. From the kind of knowledge that builds itself up as a response to one's needs, curiosity, research and intuition, there is a gradual shift, as the process progressively becomes institutionalised, towards information that is rapidly consumed, within learning spaces that are far off from the places that succeeded in generating mechanisms and pathways responsible for all the instruments we have available and that we use, no longer aware of what they mean. The physical environment designated for education has clearly diversified from those 'unconscious learning' spaces, taking the shape over time of an environment entrusted with deliberate teaching. The school building has become the everyday environment where children pass their crucial years, with lasting effects on their lives. School has a long-lasting physical structure, where processes of transmission and development of the cultural heritage take place through the succession of generations of children and educators: it therefore needs planning that can neither be serial nor casual. As Silvano Tagliagambe suggests, a learning environment cannot correspond to the classroom (a physical space), or even less the class (a prevalently administrative unit); it must, rather, take shape as a place whose first objective is to succeed in fostering the involvement and participation of the students, to encourage their capacity to build up cognitive pathways 'adjusted' to their own abilities, interests and learning pace. It is a matter of imagining places able to stimulate knowledge building instead of spaces structured for simple reproduction or transmission. It should be remarked, however, that school classrooms are rarely configured to stimulate processes of collaboration and interaction between teachers and learners, be it by encouraging reflection and reasoning or by suggesting problems and contexts arising from the real world.

Research paths
Over the last few years the research work the ecourbanlab has carried out at the Department of Architecture, Design & Urban Planning in Alghero has focused on the theme of design for learning spaces, with the aim of exploring the contributions architectural planning can offer to build up a learning environment aimed at achieving specific didactic objectives. The various activities promoted by this research have led to verifiable results as concerns the construction of such spaces but the need remains to identify new methodologies.

The key role has emerged, among the research conclusions, of the relationship between brain-body and built space in learning processes, as an outcome of the discovery of mirror neurons, which appear to phenomenologically define the empathic relationship with the world. These neurons are called 'mirror' neurons as they activate, in the neural system of an individual observing a certain behaviour, a specular reaction to the action observed; in other words, with neural circuits we simulate others' actions, in the same areas of the brain that we use to carry out our actions, often in an unconscious or even precognitive manner. Seeing an object automatically recalls the action connected with it, just as observing another's behaviour means, for the brain, to simulate the corresponding potential action. The body thus plays a fundamental role in developing each individual's mental representation, which will change continuously during life, so that we become different depending on what we do and learn. Motor disciplines show how children very quickly learn to imitate the movements of athletes' bodies, observing, for example, how they hit or kick a ball, so that by activating mirror neurons, they simulate the athletes' muscular dynamics. As they grow, they acquire skills through verbal teaching, but even more through the transfer of the teacher's muscular activity directly to the learner, through sense perception and body imitation. The mirror neuron empathic system is not limited to the sense of sight; we constantly understand and learn with all our senses, building up a sense of belonging to a space, place and community. Action is the essential element to achieve any learning; a space adequate for this purpose must be able to favour the process.

Another research outcome concerns the need to build spaces characterised by emotional and multisensory experiences, within which experiments with body actions can take place that are indispensable for the development of cognitive processes. Body movement is actually taken into consideration almost exclusively in sports and dancing activities, whereas senses like hearing and sight are recognised only in direct connection with artistic or musical disciplines, while whole body existence is rarely identified as the foundation of the learning capacity.

From this point of view, Juhani Pallasmaa is one of the architects that have mostly emphasised the role of the senses in our way of conceiving, teaching and analysing architecture, also and above all in school building design. In one of his best known and most influential books, "The eyes of the skin", he maintains that the majority of contemporary schools do not manage to sufficiently stimulate the senses, because the spaces they contain concentrate mainly on visual perception. Contemporary schools are largely characterised by a set of static, poorly stimulating environments, in some ways alien to the primary process of knowledge triggered by everyday sensory stimuli. Pallasmaa claims that, apart from sight, the other senses have a role, especially touch, in the experience and understanding of the world; he considers all the senses an extension of touch, i.e. different ways of 'touching' the world, the most authentic essence of life experienced. On these assumptions it is indispensable to think of spatialities measurable through sight, movement, touch, smells, namely, with the co-presence of sensations able to relate complete body perception with built environment: «An architectural work is not experienced –writes Pallasmaa–as though it were a series of isolated retinal figures, but in the complete integration of its material, bodily and spiritual essence.»

The building in question envisages multisensory experience of architectural space, able to link together structure, sound, temperature, material consistency of surfaces, internal objects, tension between inside and out, cosiness and, last but not least, light: a set of components, each different but indispensable, giving life to the sensations Peter Zumthor considers essential to create an 'atmosphere'. It is actually in the atmosphere generated by a quality environment that the value should be assessed of a construction built with skilful use of materials and spaces to convey sensations. This concept is explored further by Zumthor in *"Atmospheres"*, the transcription of a lecture he gave at the Castle of Wendlinghausen during a Festival of Music and Literature. Atmosphere is the unit of measure by which an architectural work is judged, becoming an aesthetic category: «I am passionate about architecture, but the atmosphere, empty spaces, the physical and tactile experience of a building are enough for me. I need nothing more. If we lose sight of the beauty of architecture we are left just with images, and an image is not a building.» The concept at the base of atmosphere in architecture for Zumthor is the fact that men and things influence each other: «This is the theme I am facing as an architect. And I believe my passion for architecture lies precisely in this theme. There is magic in reality. As an architect I ask myself: what is the magic of reality? A photo Baumgartner took (in the thirties), in the café of a student hostel. Those men sitting at tables; and they are contented.» Zumthor wonders: «Am I able, as an architect, to design atmospheres like these? Am I able to produce the same intensity and consistency? And if so, in what way? The materials, sounds, smells, together with the light and objects are a fundamental part of this atmosphere and build up the material presence of the building, turning the space into a live element, into 'an authentic body to touch'.»

To understand the role and importance of a multisensory environment in learning processes it is useful to go back to Pallasmaa, when he talks about the years of his education in a school in the Finnish countryside. «I can still remember the smell of my first day at school 65 years ago. It was during the war years; I had been taken from the town where we lived to my grandfather's in the Finnish countryside. I went to a rather simple school but in some ways the education was forward-thinking. In those times, the students of an agricultural community took turns going to school at 6.30 in the morning, before the other students arrived at 8.30, to light the fire in the stove to heat the school. Looking back, I appreciate those dark mornings in the cold school building. It created the feeling that the school was not just an abstract place for learning, but an integral part of life. The smell of burnt wood and the soap used to wash the wood flooring: those smells were for me the essence of the school.» The story helps us to see that it is possible to improve learning abilities when one is strongly rooted in one's life experience, where tastes and smells can also become reference points and places of memory.

Educational environments need to manifest spatial and sensorial conditions able to root children in real life. Children of all ages need spaces where they can learn by touching, handling, 'making things' with their hands. Consistent with the discoveries of neuroscience, which show the correlation between motor patterns and cognitive functions, spatiality is needed that is able to provide opportunities for action. In this process the senses are the primary instrument for developing learning connected with the complex sequence both of movements and of time-space relations necessary to carry out a task. The way to activate the senses needs to be found, through design that is able to manage sound, smell, taste, touch and memory of movement, creating environments full of sensory experience that will help students to keep and retrieve what they learn. Going back to the body and its sensations means reclaiming a common sense to make school more human and liveable.

From the verification that spaces have an impact on individuals' moods and efficiency a further research result emerges achieved by the ecourbanlab, namely the need to design schools that generate good doses of empathy; this was reached thanks also to a series of teaching activities, such as the ILS Summer Schools which, in their four editions from 2016 to 2019, experimented with operating methods and modalities to design learning space. A school that has an empathic character must necessarily take shape as a set of spaces able to involve the different senses. These spaces should have form and colour, apart from a tactile dimension, and be able to foster reciprocity between environment and learning for the wellbeing of pupils and teachers. The need to plan scholastic spaces as emotional and multisensory experiences, essential for the development of cognitive processes, cannot leave aside the awareness that interiors must also have sound qualities. It is not simply a question of adopting some acoustic solutions, but of considering the modulation of echoes as an opportunity for many sound experiences and, consequently, for a variety of uses of the rooms.

Real space/virtual space
A basic misunderstanding characterises the relationship between the contemporary school building and new technologies. It is clear that opportunities are offered by recent progress in the field of construction materials, such as thermoregulation in rooms, and by renewable energy, but also by the new information and communication technology, and it is necessary that these find room and use in teaching processes. It is also clear that it has not really been understood how to fully exploit these opportunities. The advantages offered by the innovations can only be applied by radically rethinking the organisational and spatial models of the learning environment. Problematic cases are: computers, often relegated to special classrooms or computer labs completely alien to the process of socialisation in teaching; LIM interactive multimedia boards, used mostly in classes as an updated version of the old blackboard, but poorly compatible with the pedagogical theories the majority of teachers claim they believe in. The partial and limited use of LIMs does nothing more than enhance the traditional teacher-centred teaching model, without stimulating investigation, curiosity or groupwork. This error is linked with the difficulty of understanding the new technologies in teaching processes, to which just the assimilation of the network paradigm would suffice, i.e. distributed intelligence, which materialises in the Internet. Traditional individual learning could (and should) be enriched with collective and connective learning processes, enhancing the skills of discussion and communication, also via the conscious use of the opportunities offered by the global network. Why not imagine environments characterised by

interactive multimedia tables, for example, where each student can work and interact in a collective, collaborative process? From these considerations another ecourbanlab research outcome emerges, which can be summarised in the need to imagine spaces with a new, open, flexible conception, no longer bound to the traditional class lesson: spaces structured to favour learning linked with socialisation, cooperation and collaboration between groups of pupils and between pupils and teachers; spaces amid real and virtual, able to promote the exchange of information, communication and knowledge. Contemporary school buildings need an extension of the concept of place of learning, imagining physical environments that can accommodate unlimited quantities of virtual environments able to enhance them and put them online. Learning environments should expand, integrating artificial and virtual reality in the physicality of a school, wanting to enable its pupils to critically master the wide range of cognitive potential they have available without preventing the use of materials and technologies to make it efficient, pleasant and comfortable.

The contributions the Focus Groups of the 2016 ILS Summer School collected actually point out the importance of innovations in energy, technology and safety in designing school buildings. The objective stated in these moments of encounter between different disciplines is to start up a debate useful for design work: experts of the sectors then face teachers and pupils, in an attempt to understand how the different specialists can interact. Studies aimed at implementing and developing ICT technologies, for example, are moving in this direction, indicating a dual opportunity: to improve the interiors (in terms of microclimate conditions, brightness, temperature, functionality and safety, etc.), but also provide devices and applications with didactic-educational goals. As for the building's 'wrapping', many examples have been shown that demonstrate the importance of passive energy-saving techniques, with special attention to the possible synergy between materials and 'wrapping' construction technologies and the space-volume configuration, able to considerably reduce energy consumption both in new builds and buildings to be renovated. To recover and adapt the existing building patrimony, above all in Italy, a further objective is placed —seismic retrofitting - linked with the vulnerability typical of the static-constructor features of buildings now outdated. Here it is a matter of defining elements of technological innovation coherent with the architectural and energy aspects of the building, resorting, for example, to a modular structural scheme, seismically effective, that could take part in defining the architectural and plant solutions without being an element of contrast but of integration in designing learning space.

Internal spatiality should, also and above all, be conceived and organised through the functional and perceptual qualities of the materials. Planning comfort in school environments is a pedagogical necessity that corresponds to the natural need for well-being, improving the standards of living of those who spend a large part of their time there. It should not be forgotten that the interior of a school building also communicates: like the external elevations, it is able to recount and reverberate, by means of the different spatial configurations and surface variations. The need for careful attention also to the acoustic qualities of school buildings has already been emphasised; it is worth insisting on the fact that this aspect should not be limited to a generic acoustic solution but needs different solutions relating to the qualities envisaged for the various environments. Depending on needs and activities, communication may take on higher or lower tones, also depending on those present. The configuration of the environments and use of materials should be combined with respect for echo modulation, envisaging changing sonorous experiences according to the activity.

The development of Internet has caused an unprecedented change from an industrial society to an information society and the arrival of the digital era has radically transformed the physical world too, especially the way in which we live together. The digital revolution has also caused a new way of thinking and managing knowledge, which did not precede the new technologies but was brought on by them, following the thesis expressed by Michel Serres in "It's not a world for old people. Why youngsters are revolutionising knowledge". This analyses the *forma mentis* of the new generations: free access to information will give the majority of people the opportunity, for the first time in history, to build up their own learning landscape. In the newspaper "Repubblica", in an article titled "Dalla parte dei nuovi bambini inventiamo un'altra educazione per gli studenti Pollicino" (On behalf of the new children we are inventing a different kind of education for Thumbelina students), Serres recalls that «without us realising it, and in a short period of time (between our days and the Seventies) a new kind of human being has been born. This boy or girl does not have the same body or life expectancy of the preceding ones; they do not communicate in the same way, do not perceive the same world, do not live in the same nature or inhabit the same space.» The French philosopher has affectionately nick-named these digital natives Thumbelinas, due to their ability to write messages with their thumbs at lightning speed. These different Thumbelinas will no longer devote themselves to the occupations of the past; their conception of space is different, thanks to the cell-phone, GPS and the net and they also need to imagine new relationships, as the spread of social networks witnesses. The questions Serres poses about the future can be resumed in three main ones: What should be conveyed? To whom? In what manner? His answer is symptomatic of the difficulties of the current world of education: «What should be conveyed? Knowledge? Here it is, everywhere, on the net, available, objectivised. Should it be conveyed to everyone? All knowledge is now accessible to anyone. How should it be conveyed? No sooner said than done. By access to persons and the accessibility of any place, knowledge is now within everyone's range. In some ways it has already been conveyed, always and everywhere. Objectivised, but above all disseminated. Not concentrated. We feel an urgent need of this radical transformation of teaching, though we are still far from it.»

In the contemporary world, knowledge is everywhere, externalised, accessible. Nevertheless, the fact is surprising that a teacher no longer manages to obtain the silence and attention of a class for the lesson; Serres wonders why on earth a class should give him/her it, if with a click they can obtain the same content, in a form that is even more in-depth, contextualised, linked with what it is related to? The teacher's precise knowledge in class proves to be ridiculous and dreary, for the passiveness of listening is tedious and it bores Thumbelinas. Serres expects everything will be reinvented. New (or perhaps old) spaces should be imagined so that they can be interconnected, within which the understanding and advice of older generations might reduce the excesses of distributed knowledge, decentralised, mobile and interconnected, to keep what is good in the old system and integrate different conceptions to the benefit of everyone.

The city inside the school

It therefore seems necessary to challenge the principles that have until now built up learning spaces. On the one hand, it is a case of reconsidering the places traditionally assigned to teaching, starting with the official or institutional nature of the school building, to continue with developing new configurations for other environments traditionally entrusted with this purpose, the classroom, auditorium, laboratory... and so on. On the other, it is a question of challenging also the role and space of other places of informal learning, the corridor, courtyard, canteen, public space, etc. This reconfiguration might not, however, be sufficient. If schools are no longer exclusively in charge of education, they must necessarily redefine their function, promoting synergies with the city with the aim of activating new ways of learning. Places of education are now perceived as everyday spaces: not just dedicated, confined environments as schools are, but spaces generating closer links with the world, according to models based on the genesis of complex interactions. School buildings could take shape as places of encounter and relations between individuals, as central hubs of a connective learning fibre spread throughout the city. Urban dynamics could widen the opportunities for learning, via a mixture of inside and outside the building, reabsorbing and unifying the characteristics that distinguish them. The interior could incorporate the city, opening its spaces to uses shared and compatible with the taught work, with a transversal nature of actions able to involve the physical context and the community, to the point of turning the school into an urban fragment. Many school building functions (like the library, gym or auditorium) have the possibility of hybridising their use, opening up to external users and expressing a condition of belonging to a vaster community. The school building's relationship with the city can therefore be reappraised, creating a possible sequence that from public space passes to shared space to arrive at that safe, protected one of the scholastic enclosure; a rereading of the school «as a community space above all in a time of growing social complexity and differences between co-present languages and cultures.» Much more than other buildings, the school may become a place recognised and inhabited by a community, linked together by sentiments of belonging and common objectives.

From this point of view, the meaning of *user* of an architectural work takes on importance, long considered a source of information for planning. In some ways, the choice of the term *user* was part of the functionalist paradigm between the two World Wars: «It was said that if a relationship existed between buildings and human behaviour, then it was necessary to have a word to represent those upon whom it was considered the buildings acted. The term *user* filled this need, providing the second required variable in the functionalist equation. Hence, the user could be seen as the result of the functionalist model.» Another definition of the term characterised the decades following the end of the Second World War, in which architecture was an instrument for establishing relations between capital and labour, with buildings for users convinced of their 'equal' social value; these buildings tried to level out important social differences by simulating 'equal' spaces. For many architects of the second half of the last century it was necessary to convince themselves and the public that the true commissioner of public buildings was not those who had effectively commissioned them, but those were to inhabit them.

School-user-community

The close link between inhabitant and architecture, driven by a process of participated appropriation on the part of users, was featured in the work of some architects who made it the hallmark of their style. One of the most interesting is Herman Hertzberger; in all his projects, but above all those for schools, he has always tried to offer users a high degree of transformability and modification of spaces, without wanting to completely foresee the uses. «The translation of the concepts *public* and *private* in terms of differentiated responsibilities —writes Hertzberger—makes it easier for the architect to establish in which areas elements need to be put in place that will allow the 'users/inhabitants' to contribute to the environmental project and in which areas this is less important. In organising a floor plan, at the moment the plan and section are designed and also on the basis of the "principle for installations", the conditions may be created for a greater sense of responsibility and consequently also for greater involvement in the organisation and furnishing of an area. Only then will the users become inhabitants.» The chapter "From user to inhabitant" of Hertzberger's "Lessons for Students in Architecture" begins thus. The Montessori School he designed in Delft was one of the buildings chosen to try to give shape to the metaphor of an urban landscape composed of a series of 'little houses', represented by classrooms, placed along a common street, represented by the hall. The teacher was entrusted with the task of defining, together with the children, the domestic shape and atmosphere of the interior. The school spaces at Delft therefore try to express educational principles based on fulfilling domestic duties, with the objective of strengthening the children's emotional affinity with the context. The spatial structure deployed by Hertzberger enabled the pupils to become inhabitants, making the 'school-home' environments (classrooms) homely with elements of everyday home life, like plants placed in suitable niches or by exhibiting their manual work in showcases. This form of appropriation allows pupils to be an active part in the construction of environments in which they identify themselves as members of a community.

In other school projects, too, Hertzberger developed the same design elements, able to cope with contemporary problems by configuring flexible environments in relation to the uses and features the individual user (pupil) wished to organise within them. To break with the closed nature of the traditional classroom, work could be done on the space around the class, to then continue into the connecting space, providing it with shelving, niches, worktops and corner seats. A transition area is thus generated that belongs both to the class and to the corridor and can be interpreted in terms of the context. The connecting space turns into a multiple space with a clearly urban character, as in the "Montessori College Oost" in Amsterdam, but one also able to accommodate places of work and promote spontaneous activities, shown, for example, by the presence of ICT workstations spread along the entire gallery of the Titaan school hall in Hoorn.

The "Montessori College Oost" also develops around a central space set out on different levels, into which all the activities external to the classrooms converge. The analogy with urban space is clear: a public space is evoked overlooked by the galleries of the various environments surrounding it; an open system and social space able to favour a variety of experiences and take on many meanings, in which the aspects and opportunities linked with learning are clearly accessible.

In his second book dedicated to the relationship between space and learning, Hertzberger summarises the concepts that for him are fundamental to demonstrate how a space can stimulate and encourage learning. Taking the teaching space outside the classroom, so that it expands into the building, is essential to build up an alternative to the closed teaching within the classroom walls and to begin to work on connective spaces, creating places that can be inhabited by the individual and groups. This is space without order or hierarchies, it is a 'whole' in motion, able to absorb and interpret changes that Hertzberger defines as "Learning Landscape", a structure whose flexibility is the balance between places set aside for individual study and collective environments able to accommodate groups and common activities. The organisation of these connective spaces is very important, for the more it is structured the richer it will be in opportunities and meaning, as a real alternative to the class system; moreover, connective spaces seem to be able to respond to the need to integrate ICT opportunities. The new theories on education, Hertzberger states, require a greater number of workspaces, diversified and individualised, separate and distinct in the space. The school building can therefore offer harmony between spaces dedicated to concentration (the individual space) and connective spaces (where collective action develops).

Going back to the Montessori school in Delft, the zones with different qualities (cosiness, openness) lie on staggered levels, so as to protect those concentrating on their work all the more; low down and close to the entrance are those engaged in noisy activities, at a higher level those who need more isolated spaces. It is therefore necessary to design learning environments where groups and individuals can work simultaneously, anticipating spaces sufficiently sheltered for each to concentrate on their work, but at the same time sufficiently open to prompt the students to interact with others. The corridor space, normally plain and empty, completely devoid of any appeal, is the first place to address for such a transformation.

Hertzberger's De Spil Polyfunctional Centre (two elementary schools, a day nursery, an infants' school, district centre and sports services) is also structured like an urban zone. The location of the complex, on the edges of a park close to the Malburgen-west district, was an important departure point for planning. Next to a single block with an elongated shape, with the two schools and day centre, a second facility with public activities for the district was programmatically separated from the first by a glass hallway at different levels. All the parts of the complex can be accessed from the central block, which looks like a town square, bustling with activity; the U-shape of the stairway encourages children to sit in a semi-circle and, altogether, the centre expresses a sense both of community and of freedom for each one to walk and move around.

The same criterion is revisited at the only school building created in Italy by Hertzberger, in the Romanina district of Rome, in the diversification of spaces deployed inside and outside the building. The ten classrooms of the elementary school and six classrooms of the secondary school are set out following a functional logic, along an axis that tries, like a street, to take the shape of a sequence of common spaces, places to meet and join up for the school users. Along this 'public' axis there is a common canteen, the school theatre, open courtyards and access to the gym. This sequence makes explicit the metaphor of the street adopted by Hertzberger in designing connective spaces at different levels of the school. The canteen space may be closed by mobile walls, to respond to Italian health and hygiene regulations, but remains a multi-use space, able to accommodate many activities when the walls are open. For example, its section, being slightly lower than the connective spaces, enables people to sit along the two long sides, which feature wood-covered steps. The free central space, as well as being able to host public events, can also be used as an ideal space for the break between lessons or for collective lessons with several classes. Hertzberger was very keen for the theatre space, not envisaged in the initial programme, to follow the stratagem of enlarging the connecting stairway between the two levels of the school. The word 'stairway' is actually incorrect to denote this connective element between two levels which is a space available for theatrical productions, collective lessons, end-of-year shows, parent meetings or simply for a stop between one lesson and another or during break. The courtyards also contribute to dividing up the main axis: as possible extensions of the teaching space in the open, they are available as places to stop or meet, depending on the different kinds of use. The building features a simple support system, made up of reinforced concrete beams at a right angle to the main axis. These will enable future expansion of the building and possible changes in the internal layout, following a modular logic able to generate flexible environments in relation to use.

The reciprocal relationship between user and form can be likened to that between individual and community: «users launch themselves into the shape —says Hertzberger— just as individuals show their true colours in their variety of relations with others while interacting, and therefore become what they are.»The school may also (and above all) become the interpreter through its forms of the educational needs of a developing individual, for whom spaces are understood as places preparing for possible situations of collective interaction, rather than spaces thought up solely for the acquisition of notions; places giving a taste of gusts of common life, anticipating what the student might face outside school. School building spaces need, therefore, to be imagined as 'places' where individual learners can recognise themselves as active parts of a community: changing spaces, anticipating complex urbanity, open to social aggregation phenomena, rather than the common models of our school system which, as Francesco Dal Co recalls, are often destined to carry out «a central role in the progressive process of deterioration in ways of civil cohabiting and, even more, in fostering the harsh way mechanisms of social exclusion operate.» 'Inhabiting school', in adequate spaces and place, may become the metaphor of our 'being in the world', learning to relate to others and obey rules, taking care of the space we are immersed in and belong to. The spatial component of education proposed by Hertzberger in the "Romanina school" reveals an ethical foundation that still struggles to find appropriate models to cope sufficiently with the problems of current scholastic education. Schools today cannot escape the process of non-participation in schooling, and the urge to turn educational institutes into learning houses, or better learning cities: «a school should be like a city where you feel at home.»

Urban learning spaces

The experience Hertzberger has acquired confirms how important the type of architecture is for learning environments that will foster processes of cooperation and sharing. Numerous pedagogical studies have acknowledged space as an identity reference point in human experience, able to influence behaviour and determine cognitive processes. Space should be capable of providing opportunities for use and transformation that the individual will accept, via his own cognitive system, on the basis of a sort of bet on the future of that space. It is therefore possible to imagine places of education occupied not just inside school buildings, but also outside them.

We must nevertheless be aware of the substantial difference between 'quantity' and 'quality' of urban amenities in cities and their tangible capacity to accommodate action projects requested by the single inhabitant or groups. The city is still considered a privileged place where the social space of the public sphere is developed, but the actual difficulty lies in singling out new events in the public sphere, in the light of the profound cultural and social transformations of contemporary times. In current public space a constant tension is recognised between the spatial dimension of everyday life and the non-space of information and the new communication technologies.

In 1977, twenty-five years after anticipating, in his article *The mechanical bride,* the nascent megalopolises as an "electronic global village", Marshall McLuhan wrote a school manual (helped by his son Eric and assistant Kathryn Hutchon), addressing high school students, with the provocative title: "City as classroom". The main purpose of the manual was to stimulate young people's curiosity, leading them to collect materials and data useful to reconstruct an urban universe characterised by the presence of the *media*. McLuhan wanted young pupils to get out of school building enclosures, in order to promote collaboration as an antidote to individualism. The research he suggested was to be conducted in the field, using audio and video instruments with the aim to contribute to a collective project. Participated observation in urban dynamics is to be wished for today as then, in order to understand the city –in its deepest logics and mechanisms–as a media environment. Contemporary metropolitan space presents itself through new methods of use, new forms of transmission of knowledge, new desires, new needs, new aspirations: a level of social complexity hard to manage with traditional instruments of education and communication, which shows the structural inadequacy of the education systems. McLuhan's provocative point of view overturned many experiments in alternative pedagogy in the second half of the nineteen-hundreds, inspired by the opposition between 'within' the school (positive) and 'outside' in the world (negative).

McLuhan imagined that the students, no longer prisoners of the dividing walls or constricting social formulas, would be encouraged to build up aggregations founded on shared collective aims, to thus also enable individual exploration of new contexts beyond the boundaries of the school building. Contexts where everyone could manage his/her own growth and learning (together with those working, studying, playing and enjoying urban places in their complexity and completeness), discovering, or perhaps rediscovering, different places and spaces with educational potential in their architectural, urban, historic and cultural features.

The basic presupposition was that urban reality may be understood as an enormous platform able to supply endless opportunities for investigating, examining, exploring. Every concrete situation contains inexhaustible educational potential for those wanting to learn to 'be in the world', observing it, discovering and inhabiting it, making it their own directly with their body and through their senses. It is not a matter of educational paths like 'excursions' organised by the traditional scholastic educational machine, but rather of free tracks, made up of manifold observations able to provide increasingly detailed fields of experience. In his book "Incidental education", Colin Ward, too, proposed informal instruction as an alternative to structured, programmed learning: roads and streets, meadows and woods, school-bus and school baths, craft shops and workshops turn into vital places, able to give extraordinary educational opportunities. Ward's glance mainly addressed the many everyday aspects of social life, starting with the premise that there is no circumstance that does not present a latent degree of freedom or enable a choice between "authoritarian" and "libertarian" solutions. From this point of view, education takes on a central role for its social transformation project. In the various chapters of "Incidental education" a series of examples can be found that aim to demonstrate how the unusual, creative use of the environment is the only way towards true education. On the contrary, the traditional school with its closed, fenced-in spaces proves to be too much of a closed cage for true cultural enrichment, as it proves alien to the social life of the new generations. In Ward's view, education is principally linked with the dual meaning the term 'environment' can have. On the one hand, Ward chooses the environment, meant as a context, as the only educational space, in conflict with the school classroom; on the other he claims the need for education that will concern the natural environment. True interpretation of the environment takes place only through direct contact and not by virtual representation in a classroom. For Ward, environmental education aims to explore the social context, starting with specific problems, to make children masters of their environment, including the city where the large majority of children live and attend school. Children's research should develop within the urban environment, through authentic fieldwork where they can rediscover "street experience" that has disappeared from the everyday life of young people. Contemporary society in tries to keep them as far away from the street as possible, considering it dangerous –like other urban spaces–and causing, in actual fact, detachment between young citizens and the urban reality in which they live. Ward configures an approach (simultaneously new and old) to the transmission of knowledge able to provide an effective response to that curiosity, that natural, spontaneous need to learn that is at the base of authentically libertarian education. In its different definitions, libertarian pedagogy attempts to challenge the education issue, removing the disciplinary boundaries and borders with other disciplines and other bodies of knowledge to propose educational models that have a strong antihierarchical, evolutive value. The assumption behind the approach of libertarian pedagogy is the awareness that the school could be improved and reformed, but it does not tend to implement basic structural changes. Some radical thinkers, such as Ivan Illich, took non-participation in schooling as a fundamental theme. Some fifty years ago, Illich set down his alternative view in "Deschooling society", where he proposed the kind of education that could give man back the pleasure of inventing, creating and experimenting with his own life, taking part in the challenge of liveability of the planet. Beyond the good intentions of educators, compulsory schooling (like other total institutions) reproduces the social system; it teaches individuals to measure and quantify knowledge, but also themselves, on the basis of bureaucratic parameters; it does not produce the need for knowledge but for different schooling; it teaches individuals to submit to society and prepares man for a programmed world. School is the main mechanism of social conservation and reproduction of the system; education is detached from the world and becomes anti-educational.

Ecourbanlab has acquired further awareness in its research: places of education are no longer solely environments devoted and confined to schools, but spaces able to generate closer links with the outside world, namely everyday life spaces based on the genesis of complex interactions. To intervene in planning urban space would mean to responsibly rethink the role space covers in the dynamics of the processes of use and appropriation of the city, as personal pathways of action and knowledge. The aim of the research developed at the ILS 2017 Summer School *Urban Learning Spaces* was to identify one or more spaces within the city that maintain such latent potential; we tried to reveal and strengthen them from the design point of view, recognising their role of public space as an urban learning space. A theatre, a garden, a square, a church, a museum (for example) maintains within itself features that, if appropriately reread from a design point of view, can turn these places into tools for growth of knowledge, in relation to specific qualities often not immediately or spontaneously legible. This means not losing the sense of school —to be reread (especially for the youngest) as 'home', in the etymological meaning of protection, reference point —but opening activities to the outside, making use of all occasions of experience in the urban context and places that structure it. Why not give an art lesson in a museum? Why not tell a story in a media library? Attend an open lesson in a theatre or simply play, learning in a square? Carry out-group activities in a park or read the functioning mechanisms of a company? And further, study a product watching it being made.

The principle is to keep the city in the city: some urban spaces maintain their identity and link up —in the open space via networks, infrastructures, green spaces—with the architectures of the city. Moving towards a critical reconstruction, that will choose to restore rather than eliminate, the result could take the shape of a network of 'active spaces', affected by gradual levels of project intervention. In this sense it is possible to reread the city as a great potential learning space: a space of stimulation to act and a bringer of knowledge, for an 'urban platform of connective learning'.

MF

Extended school De Opmaat, Arnhem (2004-2007)

Raffaello primary and secondary school, Rome, Italy (2005-2012)

"The architect must see and be able to see; he must know how, in which context and with ho many human difficulties his work is accomplished"

Giovanni Michelucci

CHAPTER FIVE

Innovative all-inclusive school North Area. Palermo
The classrooms

chapter five

Symbolic and functional over time

Schools and educational buildings are places where generations meet, where past and future get in contact; places of transmission, interpretation and (re)invention, in which the physical configuration both incorporate and generate symbolic rituals and systems. These rituals and systems are defined at the time of the project and during the construction, and they become the scenery, the background of relations and "taming actions" taking place during the life of the building and of people meeting there. The monumental stairways marking the entrance of "temples of culture", to be found in several high-school architectures, today paired by ramps and elevators, led to spaces once "protected" by porters in uniform inside their lodges (sometimes still present and wearing a badge), or later guarded by posts through which students had to swipe their badge, before geolocation by smartphone made all these rituals useless, even allowing the parents to be notified by Whatsapp of the students' absence from school.

Nursery schools and kindergarten located at ground floor, surrounded by trees, with large panel windows and bowers between outside and inside, typical of the more recent neighborhoods, have generally barrier-free access and multiple spaces where caregivers and children can meet, set up with colorful and creative signage explaining activities and educational projects.

Therefore, the mere act of entering school represents, communicates and makes possible different ways and functions of relations, and implies diverse "conceptions" of the place, of its value and significance. These conceptions are incorporated in the buildings' structures, which implicitly influence and connote the meaning of educational experience in that place, designing its *genius loci*. The same can be said of all sort of places developing inside schools.

The awareness of the intertwining of functional and symbolic dimension, growing both in education and in architecture and urban sciences, emerges and is expressed in a synchronic key when "new" schools are planned. When the functional and economic criteria prevail, the paradigm, the timeless "archetype" focus on the classroom and its possible configurations, in modules or clusters, as exemplified in temporary schools built after earthquakes in Italy, or in the models and strategies oriented to the planning of standard school modules suitable for various combinations. When the social, civic and participation criteria prevail, planning aims at individuating the features of a "collectively desired" school, focusing on the "here and now", as it can be seen in the integrations of school buildings in educational/community centers and campuses, especially in low-density towns where the school acts as a "garrison" of protection of the community against social disintegration and depopulation. A third option is a future-driven (and sometimes utopian) perspective, aiming to plan the "school of tomorrow, for the new millennium" etc. In this case, imagination designs and builds contexts which are desired and desirable especially by their own planners.

The consequences of these "synchronic" approaches can be summarized as follows: with the first approach, the reiteration of a model that fatally absorbs and reduces to itself every attempt of renewal (as showed by the resistance of the "forme scolaire" to all technological innovation); with the second approach, the quick obsolescence and the continuous need for adaptation and restructuring made necessary by the changes in contexts; with the third the inability to meet expectations, needs and abilities of the end users – especially teachers and local stakeholders -, suggesting changes and sometimes the abandonment of spaces, when the "future" has been enacted in forms too different from the one envisaged and desired by the users. In all cases, educational places must confront themselves with "outdatedness" as a problem and possibility. This implies the necessity of a diachronic glance, inspired to educational relations, in the design, planning and reading of places dedicated to formal education and learning processes.

Not only "space", but also "time" is a generator of educational places. Both must be considered in their dimensions and components, with a stereoscopic perspective including and combining storytelling and paradigms. Places are indeed spaces that generate, host and narrate stories, experiences, encounters, relations: as far as schools are concerned, all this is about education.

Therefore, schools are conceived as places more than "non-places" to be traversed in order to reach a result, or the age of conclusion of compulsory education, or, for teachers, the desired retirement. Places like Italo Calvino's city of Eufemia, in which memories are exchanged and in which temporary residents share, enhance and transform their own history.

In this perspective, the space between the gate and the stairway is not only a former garden, transformed in reserved parking for the teacher but also an aggregating, loud space appropriated by the pupils before the bell announcing the beginning of the school day and filled by their screams and runs after the lessons. It can be thus re-generated (not only imagined and planned in an architect studio) with the participation of people from inside and outside the school, inviting them to meet there to give this space social meanings, instead of a mere role of transit, and make their relations recognizable, neither clandestine nor marginal. It is indeed, for students' life stories, an important place, like the classroom and often more than that, playing a crucial role in the building of identities and biographies.

Today this liminal space acts as a compensative space facing the virtual space of relations in social networks, whose connections continue to act "under the desk" during school hours. And tomorrow? When bionic post-humans and AI will populate the scene? Contemporary "schools of the future" will perhaps become disused land, as many industrial areas already are?

Even restricting ourselves to the 50-year life span of contemporary architecture, can we envisage that either the repetition of the "cells and drills" model will continue, or that "today's fashion" will resist, or that we are able to foresee precisely the form of and learning in the subsequent half-century? In the same schools built as a sequence of classrooms in the Sixties, now we find "tamed" technologies as interactive blackboards and digital attendance rolls; cables and curtains are added; in the meanwhile and under the desks, smartphones rule. Pupils have no difficulties to stay connected all day, while a lot of money and time is wasted for already obsolete wire connectivity and soon-to-be-ignored regulations are issued…. Sysiphean labour or mission impossible? It is certainly so, if school is conceived (both in its physical meaning and in its educational scope) as a defined, stable, mechanical context, predictable and therefore fragile, following an Assembly Line Instruction logic – still prevailing in all institutional system governed by the so-called "new public management" and implemented by the global "soft governance". But there are other, more effective ways to understand and enact school.

These ways highlight the personal and social meanings of schooling, valorize its "world of life" aspects beyond its institutional function, and recall the dynamic, evolving meeting of generations taking place in school, which promotes mutual transformation even when it is oriented to cultural transmission.

Moreover, the idea of school, its pedagogical concept and the consequent architectural planning endlessly connect with the history and function of this educational place, in its social and geographical context, following the tensions and aims of its time. Nevertheless, school is bound to transformation, because of its dealing with the young people, with social and technological change and with the work of (re)interpretation embedded in cultural transmission. Its condition is to be located between "already" and "not yet", to be open, proactive and projected as a meeting point between generations and a generative place.

Architectural planning should, therefore, emphasize both being clearly placed and rooted, and its openness: school building should be able to be easily re-structured, refitted and converted, transformed and re-generated, instead of offering "perfect", complete and final design; buildings should propose, promote and welcome ideas, instead of provoking, challenging or defining a model for the future. Sure enough, the schools of the future will define themselves gradually and following a non-linear logic.

For further illustration, a "case history" will be more effective than the introduction of definitions, paradigms and distinctions. This was the clear impression we received when we got in contact with it and, therefore, we conclude this paper with the history of LA-Balena [The Whale].

In his description of the project (1975), the architect Renato Raggi wrote: "The area in which the nursery school will be built… is part of a large area defined as public space in the most recent city planning" (the municipality of Ortonovo, renamed Luni in 2017). The municipality was located between sea and mountains; between wild forests, agricultural land and factories; at the borders of the regions Liguria, Toscana and Emilia. Its ancient past is testified by relics of Roman constructions, and its recent, tumultuous development can be clearly seen in the image provided by Google Maps half a century later:

In a context marked by individual housing development, Renato Raggi highlights the "core meaning of schools in social development […] with their compensation of inequalities […] and perspectives for development, because in schools values and interests are shared not only by pupils and teachers, but also by the families (parents) and the community as a whole". As a consequence, "the meaning of this building" is to be found both in "the construction of a complex of spaces for children up to six years of age" and in the individuation of a "place in urban context open to participation of families and of the entire community to the educational process".

Raggi drew inspiration from the ellipse, the formal and contextual archetype of the project (the ruins of the Roman amphitheatre in Luni are less than 2 kilometers far from the area) to design a nursery school, a kindergarten, a public park near the Canale Lunense without barriers and comprising a little lake, stables with cattle, greenhouses, vegetable gardens, an open-air theatre, a playground with sand and a slide, a boules court and a skating rink.

The full project was not enacted because of lack of funding. Only the nursery school was built, following evolution criteria on a children's scale of proportions. The project included open and connected closed spaces allowing the child to participate in activities according to his development, and was enriched by fantastic elements and symbolic references, both outside and inside.

"I really wanted to include in the project something that would have become its symbol and would have made clear to everybody that it was a children's center. The whale, the friendly giant of the sea, gave a more "childish" tone to the all-gray buildings… The whale, moreover, was meant to contain children's toys to be used outside, while its back was the entrance ramp between the first floor and the garden", explains Raggi (interviewed in December 2018).

In the 1975 project description, he wrote: "… backlit by the colored skylights, children will be able to observe the structural elements – pillars and beams – transfigured in 'ramifications of big trees'" to be found in the area, thus constructing "a gradual passage between closed rooms and the outside, arranging bowers in some areas…"

The building was up and running as a nursery school for around 25 years. In 2015 it was closed because of the low number of children living there and remained unused for some years without sparking any interest in the residents. The "problem of abandoned areas" had been perceived and discussed by Raggi in an essay written with Silvano D'Alto in the journal La Nuova Città (n. 6/7, 1992), founded by Giovanni Michelucci and today edited by the Michelucci Foundation.

The problem has been turned to an opportunity for the company Birimbò LAB, directed by Lisa Biso who, with Irene Moretti (both former pupils of that nursery school) has organized in recent years successful and innovative activities and educational services, involving the participation of local inhabitants. The Birimbò LAB team has elaborated a project for the reuse of the building, embraced by the municipality. Architect Raggi has been involved, giving him the opportunity to "see the full realization of the original, 50-years-old ideas and project […] to build both a new world for children and a shared community space, where education would be for all and where children would feel free to act, make attempts, and expand knowledge".

This case history highlights some aspects of the planning of learning spaces able to generate and re-generate human, social and cultural spaces, without limiting ourselves to the functional reproduction of standard (and standardizing) models. Therefore, spaces can become meaningful for people meeting there and exchanging histories of mutual improvement. This was the aim of LABoratorio, both rooted in the *genius loci* and embodying *utopian* aims proper of the participatory-emancipatory practices of the Seventies, when the first project of the building was made; of the continuous intertwining of functional dimension (the entrance ramp/toy closet, pillars and beams) with symbolic dimension (the "big trees"); of inside with outside, incorporated by LA-Balena with its concrete ramifications; of Birimbò LAB which listens to emerging needs, demands and conditions and responds to all this with new and creative educational services. An operative mode which opens new possibilities instead of reducing the planning of school buildings to a sequence of procedures and protocols.

PC

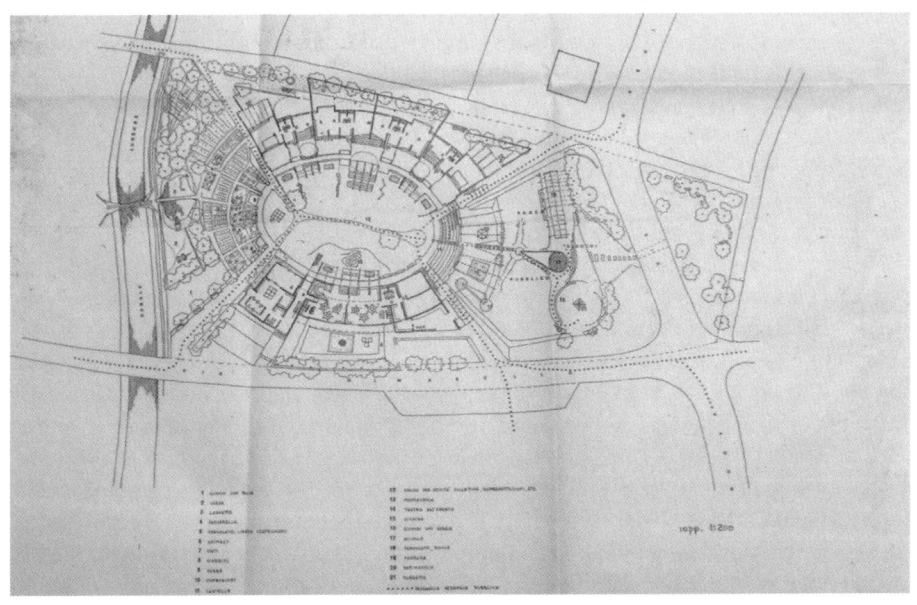

General plan of the Raggi's project (1975)

Reasoned bibliography

A synthetic bibliography on the theme of the relationship between pedagogy and school form is a difficult and complex operation both for the enormous scientific production on the subject and for the heterogeneity of the contributions that are hosted in this volume. We will therefore limit ourselves to listing the key texts that have guided the arguments of each individual text. In "the school in the middle " we describe some data on the Italian school taken from "The unique portal of school data" and then refer to the work of Prakash Nair summarized in "Blueprint for tomorrow - Redesignin Schools for Student-Centered Learning ", Harvard Education Press, Cambridge, 2014. On the topics of learning and pedagogical activism, described in" The landscape as a learning environment "see "Manuale di pedagogia didattica" by Franco Frabboni and Franca Pinto Minerva, published for Laterza, Bari, 2013. A wide discussion on the typological aspects related to the architecture of the school is contained in the chapter, edited by Ciro Cicconcelli, "Scuole materne elementari e secondarie", reported in the book by Pasquale Carbonara, "Architettura pratica", vol. 3, 2, UTET, Turin, 1958. On the historical events that characterized the theme of the school, up to the sixties of the last century, see the number of Casabella 245, 1960, which also contains the text of Aldo Visalberghi "Apertura del dibattito: per una pedagogia dell'ambiente"(pp. 44-48) and the description of the contents of the XII Triennale di Milano. The issues related to the "pedagogical role of contexts" are partly described in the text by Paola Granata " Ecologia dei media. Protagonisti, scuole, concetti chiave" editions Franco Angeli, Milan, 2015. The drawings of the elementary school of Siliqua are kept at the Museum of Modern and Contemporary Art of Trento and Rovereto (MART) - Archive of the '900, Fondo E. Sottsass sr. , "Progetto per una Scuola elementare di 8 aule a Siliqua (Cagliari)" - June 1, 1951, Sot. I.230 (1-8), Plans elevations and sections, china on gloss, scale 1: 100; Sot. I.1.230.9, Planimetry, china on gloss, scale 1: 1000 (aut. Publication of 11.23.2017). In reference to the project by Ettore Sottsass sr. and Ettore Sottsass jr. see also the short essay "Scuola Elementare a Siliqua", published in Domus 302, 1955, pp. 15-17 and the book "Per qualcuno può essere lo spazio" edited by Matteo Cadignola (edited by), Adelphi, Milan, 2017. The chapter "Spaces, places and landscapes of learning" initially refers to the work of Juhani Pallasmaa "The eyes of the skin" on the involvement of the senses in the aesthetic experience of space. On the same subject is quoted "Atmospheres" by Peter Zumthor. On the relationship between school and community some Hertzberger projects are recalled including the Montessori College Oost.

For a critical analysis of the symbolic and social functions and meanings of the school and the related adaptations over time are fundamental: Foucault M., "Surveiller et punir. Naissance de la prison ", Gallimard, Paris, 1976; Vincent G., "L'éducation prisonnière de la forme scolaire? Schooling and socialization in the societies industrielles ", Presses Universitaire de Lyon, Lyon, 1994;
Appadurai A., "Modernity at Large", University of Minneapolis Press, Minneapolis, 1996. The interaction between school devices and digital technologies is well explored, for example, in Pireddu M., " Social Learning. Le forme comunicative dell'apprendimento ", Guerini Scientifica, Milan, 2014;
Eugeni R., " La condizione postmediale", La Scuola, Brescia, 2015. The main contemporary policies of transformation of school architecture are well summarized in Borri S. (ed.), "The Classroom has Broken. Chianmging School Architecture in Europe and Across the World ", Indire, Florence, 2018. Empirical research on educational settings and their transformations can be found, for example, in the volumes that also contain the following essays Calidoni P. (2016), "Immagini dalle aule. La perdurante predominanza del modello didattico 'uno-tanti'", in the Democratic School 1/2016; Calidoni P. & Ghiaccio M.F., "The School Community re-think the learning environment", in RicercAzione, 2/2018.
To master the contents of the text we recommend reading Evans, G.W., & McCoy, J.M. (1998). When buildings don't work: The role of architecture in human health. *Journal of Environmental Psychology*, 18, 85-94; Gifford, R. (2002). *Environmental psychology: Principles and practice*. Boston: Allyn & Bacon; Sanoff, H., & Walden, R. (2012). School environments. In S.D. Clayton, (Ed.), *The Oxford Handbook of Environmental and Conservation Psychology*. New York: Oxford University Press (pp. 276–294).

Credits
······

The Iscol@ experience, within which these reflections take shape, was first and foremost a great intellectual laboratory that allowed experts from different disciplines to confront and interact. This has served the purpose to assist the public administration in the beginning of a transformation process culminating in the realization of new schools for the regional territory. The credits for having undertaken this initiative go to Alessandra Berry and Matteo Frate – appointed by the Autonomous Region of Sardinia - who guided and inspired the work of the technicians and politicians of the territory and created the necessary conditions for the success of this initiative. The framework of Iscol@ was also the occasion to highlight the work of many young architects and students who have laid the foundations of their professional success on the subject of schools and learning spaces. In these pages we have reported fragments of their wonderful work: we mention with gratitude Spaziozero, Nicholas Canargiu, Sara Montis and Daniela Corona. A graduate workshop on the theme of schools has produced interesting graduation works, of which I have the pleasure to mention, among others, that of Daniela Esu, Giulia Fulghesu, Valentina Murgia and Laura Secci. Finally I want to sincerely thank the colleagues who have contributed directly to the drafting of the third issue of this series, in particular Giovanni Battista Cocco, Massimo Faiferri, Ferdinando Fornara and his research team and Paolo Calidoni as well as, of course, Bruno Messina who embellished the text of this work with an acute and brilliant preface.

We thank Arch. Renato Raggi for having kindly consented to the presentation of the case and Dr. Lisa Biso, author of the Master's thesis in LM50 Planning and coordination of educational services at the University of Parma entitled: "Birimbò and La Balena. Project for the re-generation of a service for early childhood" (a.a. 2017-2018), which has collected and made available the documentation presented here.

* The images of Spaziozero are taken from the competition projects for the Infant School in Savogna d'Isonzo (Lorenzo Ciccu, Simone Langiu, Carlo Pisano with Elisabetta Sanna, Giuliana Pintus); the Carracci school complex in Bologna (with Nicola Melis); the Gaetano Cima di Guasila Urban Civic Campus (with Metassociati, Luca Tuveri, Elisabetta Sanna)

** The images of Nicholas Canargiu and Sara Montis are taken from the project for the "International competition for the comprehensive innovative Northern Area school complex". Palermo 2017. G.M. Chiri, B. Brendolan with N. Canargiu, D. Corona, S. Montis

*** The chapter "Psychological effects of school design" was written by Sara Manca, Veronica Cerina, Clara Carreras, Simona Sacchi, Valentina Tobia and Ferdinando Fornara

Innovative all-inclusive school North Area. Palermo
The court

carnet

FORMS OF EDUCATION
Space for contemporary teaching

Written by
Giovanni, Marco Chiri
with texts of Paolo Calidoni, Giovanni Battista Cocco, Massimo Faiferri, Ferdinando Fornara et al.,

Author
Giovanni Marco Chiri

Published by
LISt Lab
info@listlab.eu
listlab.eu

This publication has been realized with the contribution of the Autonomous Region of Sardinia in the context of the "Iscol@" project

REGIONE AUTÒNOMA DE SARDIGNA
REGIONE AUTONOMA DELLA SARDEGNA

UNIVERSITÀ DEGLI STUDI DI CAGLIARI
DICAAR
Dipartimento di Ingegneria Civile,
Ambientale e Architettura

Art Director & Production
Blacklist Creative, BCN
blacklist-creative.com

ISBN 9788898774739

**Printed & Bound
in the European Union,** 2019

Series back to basics

Prohibited total or partial reproduction of this book by any means, without permission of the author and Publisher.

All rights reserved
© of LISt Lab edition;
© of the author's texts;
© of the author's images;

Sales, Marketing & Distribution
distribution@listlab.eu
listlab.eu/en/distribuzione/

The Scientific Committee of the issues List
Eve Blau (Harvard GSD), Maurizio Carta (University of Palermo), Eva Castro (Architectural Association London) Alberto Clementi (University of Chieti), Alberto Cecchetto (University of Venezia), Stefano De Martino (University of Innsbruck), Corrado Diamantini (University of Trento), Antonio De Rossi (University of Torino), Franco Farinelli (University of Bologna), Carlo Gasparrini (University of Napoli), Manuel Gausa (University of Genova), Giovanni Maciocco (University of Sassari/Alghero), Antonio Paris (University of Roma), Mosè Ricci (University of Trento), Roger Riewe (University of Graz), Pino Scaglione (University of Trento), Claudia Battaino (University of Trento), Luca Zecchin (University of Trento).

LISt Lab is an editorial workshop, based in Europe, that works on contemporary issues. LISt Lab not only publishes, but also researches, proposes, promotes, produces, creates networks.

LISt Lab is a green company committed to respect the environment. Paper, ink, glues and all processings come from short supply chains and aim at limiting pollution. The print run of books and magazines is based on consumption patterns, thus preventing waste of paper and surpluses. LISt Lab aims at the responsibility of the authors and markets, towards the knowledge of a new publishing culture based on resource management.